DECISIVE

WEAPONS

DECISIVE

THE TECHNOLOGY THAT TRANSFORMED WARFARE

WEAPONS

MARTIN DAVIDSON AND ADAM LEVY

BBC BOOKS

This book is published to accompany the BBC television
series *Decisive Weapons*, broadcast in 1996
Executive producer: Martin Davidson
Series editor: Janice Hadlow

Published by BBC Books, an imprint of
BBC Worldwide Publishing, BBC Worldwide Limited,
80 Wood Lane, London, W12 0TT
First published 1996
© Martin Davidson and Adam Levy 1996
The moral right of the authors has been asserted
ISBN 0 563 38768 8

Set in ITC Berkeley Oldstyle and Optima
Designed by DW Design, London
Artwork by Peter Sarsons
Artwork visualization by
Ted McCausland
Colour separations by Radstock Reproductions Ltd,
Midsomer Norton
Printed in Great Britain by Cambus Litho Ltd,
East Kilbride
Bound in Great Britain by Hunter and Foulis Ltd,
Edinburgh
Jacket printed by Lawrence Allen Ltd, Weston-super-Mare

BBC Books would like to thank the following for
providing photographs and for permission to reproduce
copyright material. While every effort has been made
to trace and acknowledge all copyright holders, we
would like to apologize should there have been
any errors or omissions:
Associated Press p 98-99; Bell Helicopter p 2, 123, 133;
Bridgeman Art Library p 46; British Library p 6-7, 26-27;
Bristol Records Office p 15; © Dean and Chapter of
Westminster p 18; E.T. Archive p 10; Eye Ubiquitous
p 130; Ian Fletcher p 59; Hulton Getty Collection p 53,
70, 80-81, 118, 137, 145; Imperial War Museum p 66, 76,
79; Lambeth Palace p 31; National Portrait Gallery p 23,
43, 50; Novosti p 78; Photo Assist p 87; Press Association
p 146; Rex Features p 139, 142; Royal Collection p 38;
TRH Pictures p 60, 82, 90-91, 95, 106, 115, 134.

CONTENTS

The helicopter is the crucial visual icon for the entire Vietnam war. It represents both the romance and the failure of America's venture in Southeast Asia. The tactics of the war were adapted to its powerful capacity to transport troops. But the Vietnamese were able to turn the Huey's capabilities to their own advantage by luring the Americans into places which favoured their defeat.

The two-fingered gesture of defiance dates back to the English archers of the fifteenth century, here practising their different skills after Sunday church services.

INTRODUCTION

THERE IS OFTEN RELUCTANCE to credit the role that weapons have played in the history of war. The influence of generals or of strategy or larger economic and social forces have been the preferred means for exploring the nature of war as well as understanding specific battles. The reasons are obvious. Weapons exist to maim and kill and should be treated with reserve, not adulation. Historians such as A. J. P. Taylor, who was obsessed with the causes of war, had no interest in technology because to them it was reductive. Taylor believed that history worked on a plane

above aircraft and guns – or below them, in the form of endless mishaps and mistakes. This book, and the television series it accompanies, is an attempt to redress that balance.

We have chosen six weapons, from the Middle Ages to the present day, that were pivotal in their respective battles. Each shows that wars are won and lost by technology. Weapons are decisive. We have not, however, taken these weapons out of context. Each is decisive in a different way. At the battle of Agincourt in 1415 the longbow established the basis of modern war in the form of distanced killing. After Culloden in 1745 the bayonet remained for 200 years the corner-stone of the imperial British army. In World War Two the T-34 tank best symbolized the way the Soviets adapted to war, while the P-51 Mustang delivered the Allied coup de grâce to Germany from the air. In Vietnam, the Bell 'Huey' helicopter provided not only the dominant sound of that conflict – the distinctive whup-whup-whup of its rotor blades – but the bitterest lesson of all: that weapons that are decisive in particular battles do not always win wars. And during the Falklands conflict the Sea-Harrier proved that with improvisation and courage, technology can be made to perform in unforeseen ways.

Although each chapter turns on the technical significance of a particular weapon all of them are as much about history as war. Each provides a window onto a specific battle, dramatizing what the larger conflict was about and how it reached its resolution. War is a strange research and development laboratory. There is something brutally simple about the priorities and the issues at stake. And yet the dynamics are extraordinarily complex, dogged by luck, perversity, courage, stupidity and sacrifice in equal measure. Underlying all these, however, are the tools of war, and they too have their history.

Each of the weapons emerged from years of prior development and military experience, often as the result of earlier disasters. And each was handled by men whose lives depended on it, either in defence or in attack.

The weapons in this book also have a cultural legacy. They left their mark long after the war for which they were developed was over, either in the memories of those who used them or, in the case of the earlier ones, in the national mythology. And all of them contributed to future military development.

Wars produce powerful stories, especially when they have ended and (some of) the dust has been allowed to settle. We have picked what we think are six of the best.

Martin Davidson
Adam Levy

ACKNOWLEDGEMENTS

VARIOUS PEOPLE have collaborated in this project, not least the series editor, Janice Hadlow, co-series producer Tim Kirby and the other directors and researchers who helped make the films. They were John Farren, Paul Tilzey, David Upshal and Navid Akhtar. Mike Ibeji, who researched three of the programmes, also made significant contributions to the chapters on the T-34 and the bayonet; these chapters could not have been written without him. Sheila Ableman at BBC Books commissioned the book and never wavered in her confidence. Fay Miller, at the BBC Research Library, handled the initial blitz of research enquiries. Jean Kay and Sheila Marshall, also at the library, filled in later with their customary aplomb. Robert Hardy kindly looked over the longbow chapter; his comments were incisive and extremely helpful. Thanks also to the pilots, soldiers, veterans, historians, authors and enthusiasts who took so much trouble to talk to us in the preparation of both the book and the series. They made us realize how little we really knew. Bobby Birchall brought an elegant eye to the design and Anna Ottewill at BBC Books kept the writing on track while we were in the midst of making the actual programmes.

CHAPTER 1

THE LONGBOW

*Even if our enemies enlist
the greatest armies, my trust is in God,
and they shall not hurt my
army or myself.*

HENRY V,
ON THE EVE OF THE BATTLE OF AGINCOURT
(25 OCTOBER 1415)

*Sire, there be enough
to be slain, enough to be taken, and
enough to be chivvied away.*

DAFYDD AP LLEWELLYN,
WELSH CAPTAIN,
AFTER RECONNOITRING THE
FRENCH AT AGINCOURT

THE CHALLENGE

THE BATTLE OF AGINCOURT is lodged deep at the heart of England's history. It is a touchstone for pluck and fortitude in the face of overwhelming odds, for bravery and physical endurance. It is the story of a small army of tired and hungry men, led by an efficient and clear-sighted leader, decisively defeating a much larger and seemingly well-equipped army. It is about the victory of the British common man over the aristocracy of France, of Henry V's soldierly tactics over the divided and confused command of the French. It tells of cunning improvisation and lucky breaks, small advantages seized upon and pressed home. But it should never be forgotten that it is also the story of butchery and carnage on a massive scale.

Another factor which gives the battle its epic resonance and continued place at the centre of national myth is the vivid contrast between the weapon systems deployed by the opposing armies on the battlefield. The English longbow was a piece of wood, hewn from a yew or elm tree and strung with a piece of hemp, that shot an arrow made from ash tipped with a piece of forged metal – all in all a humble and simple weapon, but one whose mastery demanded a high degree of skill and years of disciplined practice. Against the archer and his longbow, the French deployed a massive contingent of men-at-arms, aristocratic nobles sheathed 'cap-à-pied', from head to foot, in polished steel armour. The English also had a contingent of men-at-arms and they played an important role in the battle. But it is on the level of symbolic contrast that Agincourt echoes in the imagination – wood against steel, the common soldier against the chivalric ideal, the few against the many. It is no coincidence that Laurence Olivier, in the midst of World War Two, decided, with the help of the Ministry of Information, to make Agincourt the set-piece for his film version of *Henry V*. It was a call to stand firm as the bombs fell, to hold the line, to use historical memory as a bulwark against contemporary threat. It also helped to prepare the British nation for another invasion of France – the D-Day landings.

Henry V was 26 when he ascended the throne of England in 1413. He was lean and muscular, a born athlete and fighter. His manner was elegant but slightly reserved – a French contemporary thought he looked more like a priest than a

PREVIOUS SPREAD: The battle of Agincourt was the meeting ground for two opposing weapon systems. The French knight, dressed in armour, fought the English archer and his longbow. The English were vastly outnumbered; they fielded approximately six thousand men - five thousand archers and one thousand men-at-arms. The French had at least twenty-five thousand men, most of them knights in armour. However, the English archers and their longbows won the day.

soldier. With his brown hair cut in the classic medieval pudding-basin style, the back of his neck and sides of his head shaved close, his long lantern jaw and straight nose, he seemed to embody a new-found gravitas: contemporary accounts describe his rapid transformation from young lad to serious king on his ascension to the throne. Although he seemed stern and withdrawn he was, according to historians, full of a sense of mission. He was confident of his abilities both as a soldier and as a leader.

One thing is certain; he set about the complicated logistical arrangements of preparing for an invasion of France with determination. Agincourt was the direct result of his attempts to revive English fortunes in France. Henry had intended to lay claim to lands that had been won, and then lost, since Edward III asserted his right to the French throne in 1337 and had started a series of wars with France – the Hundred Years War – that ended in 1453. In 1413 England had Calais and her hinterland in her grip, as well as Bordeaux and a large slice of land behind it and down the coast towards the south. But Edward had conquered a much larger swathe of land, which had been ceded to England in the 1360 Treaty of Brétigny and later regained by the French. It was this that Henry had his eye on, although his larger ambitions included laying claim to the French crown, which he believed was his by right of succession from his great-great-grandmother Isabella, daughter of Philip IV. Furthermore, the seizure of the English throne by Henry Bolingbroke, Henry's father, and his accession as Henry IV, was the first real break in the Plantagenet line since Henry II. The new house of Lancaster was on shaky ground when Henry V succeeded. As a clever king and leader, he recognized that adventure abroad was an effective way to avoid problems at home.

In war, planning and preparation behind the lines are as important as decisions taken at the front. Henry was a ruthless and efficient organizer and he drew upon the nation's resources with cunning and a strong dose of administrative zeal. Time-honoured precedents for raising an army for foreign expedition had evolved during the reign of Edward III and Henry, with the help of his brother, the Duke of Bedford, refined these processes. They are important, for they had a direct bearing on the type of men he was to take into the field against the French. The different compositions of the opposing armies, and the way in which they were assembled, reflects the social make-up of the armies and helps us to decipher what actually happened on the battlefield of Agincourt.

Henry raised his army through the indenture system. Once the decision to go to war was made, the king turned to his key lords and knights (also called captains), who served as a quasi-military reserve and who enlisted troops to fight for the king. As roughly three-quarters of Henry's army was made up of longbow archers, it was to these men that the captains turned. They had trained all their lives in the arts of the longbow; and the frequency of fighting during the Hundred Years War meant they were practically a professional army. The captains would return to the king and state the number of men they could bring to battle, after which a contract for service was drawn up. The king usually paid a quarter of the soldiers' wages in advance. If necessary he would use the Crown jewels as collateral; some that Henry V handed over were not redeemed for another 15 years, well after his early death in 1422. In the fifteenth century even kings had cash-flow problems.

The real check on the system was the muster where the king called together his troops, usually at the place of embarkation. It had a dual purpose. One was to gather everyone together in a formal and organized manner. The other was to determine whether the captains had fulfilled their contracts by providing men who were battle-ready. A contract could be specific about the types of soldiers and the state of their equipment:

> *Six archers, all on horseback, and well chosen men and likely persons, well and sufficiently armed, horsed, and arrayed, every man after his degree; that is to say … harness complete, with bassinet or salade with visor, spear, axe, sword, and dagger; and all the said archers specially to have good jacks of defense, salades, swords, and sheeves of forty arrows at least.*

The mustering officer would check the words against the men, the intention against the reality. If the men were poorly armed, or their equipment was faulty or shoddy, the king could reduce their wages.

Although the French also hired paid captains these *routiers* drew their men from a system of feudal levies, or forced conscription. The men-at-arms (fully armoured knights, who bore their social status and codes of chivalry proudly), and the significantly smaller number of archers and crossbowmen, were never paid in advance as their English counterparts were. As a result, they were more likely than the English to rely on those mainstays of raising food and provisions when in the field: pillage and looting. The other main difference was the proportion of men-at-arms to archers. The English could draw upon a large pool of loyal, well-trained and generally disciplined bowmen, whose good faith and trust had been cultivated for years by the military élite. Henry's great-grandfather, Edward III, had started to encourage an archer class more than 40 years earlier in 1369 with a firm legislative decree. He declared that:

> *… everyone of the said city strong in body, at leisure times or holidays, use in their recreations bows and arrows … and learn and exercise the art of shooting; forbidding all and singular on our behalf that they do not after any manner*

This image sums up the battle: the yeoman archer against the man-at-arms. A longbow is made from a single six-foot stave of wood from the yew tree. Cut properly, the wood forms a natural spring. The honey-coloured heartwood of the belly of the bow bears the compressive force while the light sapwood bends with the tensile stress. The result is a highly lethal weapon.

Incipit secdm pncap̄ de limº libri de conquestu:

apply themselves to the throwing of stones, wood, iron, handball, football, bandyball, cambuck, or cock fighting, nor other such like vain plays, which have no profit in them ...

In a sense, these archers, rather than the outlaws of contemporary films, are the historical figures who provided the template for the original Robin Hood tales. We do not know who the model for Robin Hood was, but we have a good sense of what he stood for. He was that archetypal English figure, the yeoman. He might have had a touch of the outlaw about him but he was by no means a rebel. He objected to the growing bureaucratization of that typically English symbol of liberty: the greenwood forest. As Simon Schama brilliantly points out in *Landscape and Memory*, it was the men who benefited from this bureaucracy that Robin Hood objected to: the corrupt and profiteering abbots, the enclosers and encroachers. They had interfered in an ideal arrangement – albeit one that never really existed – a free and easy exchange between yeoman and king, where each fulfilled his duty to the other and could meet without conflict and with impunity in that mythic space: the forest. Robin Hood was, in fact, a passionate conservative, a man who wanted the elements of society to return to their proper and delineated ranks and stations. He represented nostalgia rather than rebellion. And a great part of that nostalgia had to do with his weapon: the yew longbow. Agincourt had already come and gone when the different versions of the Robin Hood legend were codified in the first clutch of printed editions of the *Lytell Geste of Robyn Hode*, in the late fifteenth century. But the powerful attraction of the longbow, in Schama's phrase, 'the most traditionally English weapon of war at the dawn of the gunpowder age', was that the object itself was imbued with ideas of liberty, self-sufficiency and the steadfastness of the yeoman – all those qualities which found their apotheosis on a muddy field in France near the village of Agincourt.

The French had a different military and cultural legacy. Although both countries had experienced social unrest in the fourteenth century in the form of the Peasants' Revolt in England and the Jacquerie in France, the French rebellion had been a much more widespread and bloody affair than its English equivalent. People from country towns had gathered in mobs and ruthlessly attacked and butchered the nobility of France. Castles and houses were burnt and destroyed, knights were tortured and their wives and children raped and killed. A French chronicler of the time estimated that the number of people in rebellion was 100 000. The uprising was savagely put down by the nobility: the Captal de Buch and his cousin the Comte de Foix took on an enormous mob in the city of Meaux, defeated them, and then burnt down the whole town, killing all who had been on the side of the Jacquerie. The memory of this ran deep, and the aristocracy was extremely hesitant about arming the people.

Any study of the battle of Agincourt throws up a simple and recurring question: why had the French not learned the lessons of previous battles with the English at Crécy (1346) and Poitiers (1356)? During both of these they had experienced the power of the concerted use of archers by the English – their lethal hail of arrows had proved devastatingly effective. The answer is far from certain, but it seems that the French understood the English tactics used at Crécy – which had the men-at-arms dismounted and flanked by their archers – but misapplied them at Poitiers, when they sought to imitate this winning battle formation. The cavalry dismounted, shortened their spears and took off their riding spurs. But the French had misjudged one crucial aspect of the English tactics: the formation favoured stability and the tactics of defence but was less suited to offensive operations which depend on the power of massive impact. The device that had worked so well for the English at Crécy proved disastrous for the French when they stormed a hill at the battle of Poitiers.

According to C.W.C Oman, whose *The Art of War in the Middle Ages* first appeared in 1885, these defeats devastated the French *noblesse*. They shut themselves up in the protection of their castles and resorted to sieges, incursions and harassing attacks against the enemy – anything but open field battles. This strategy proved successful in the short run, and they were able to retake much of the ground won by the English. But it had one major implication; the French noblity had 'forgotten nothing and remembered nothing' of previous encounters on the battlefield. In other words, the chivalrous nobles, isolated in their castles, burned with the memory of their defeats but reverted to their old codes of war. They did not follow through and try to understand the strengths of the English tactics.

Perhaps Henry, newly installed on the throne of England, sensed this weakness in the French. Certainly, he perceived that France was a divided and badly run nation. The country was torn apart by factional politics and rival parties, with Charles VI as its nominal king. But Charles was getting old and his mental state was precarious. Sometimes he thought he was made of glass and was terrified that someone might touch, and therefore break, him. At other times he became violent; his attendants would grease themselves so that they could slither out from under his clutches.

Since Henry's accession to the English throne he had made diplomatic overtures to France, including the offer to marry Charles's daughter Catherine. At the same time he had sounded out the Duke of Burgundy, leader of one of the factions that jostled for power in France. But these and other attempts to regain England's French possessions had not been fruitful. It was during this period of frustrated diplomatic activity that a story arose which, although probably greatly exaggerated, is a strong indication of how the French viewed Henry at the time and how England, moving towards conflict, was fertile ground for anything that might contribute to popular war fever.

In response to his official claim to the French throne and his desire to reclaim the lands ceded in the Treaty of Brétigny, Henry received the following message from the dauphin: 'Since you are a youngster, you are sent little balls to play with and soft cushions to lie on, until one day, perhaps you shall become a man.' With the message came a box of tennis balls. Henry's measured but ferocious reply was: 'If God so wills, and my life lasts, I will within a few months play such a game of ball in the Frenchman's streets, that they shall lose their jest and gain but grief of their game.'

Although Henry's diplomacy was unsuccessful, he had, to use a modern phrase, a duel-track plan in place. From the moment he had ascended the throne, he had planned to revive the excursions into France that had brought about the glorious victories of Crécy and Poitiers. In the year of his accession he had made Nicholas Mynot master of the king's arrows in the Tower of London, and ordered new bows to be made and old ones repaired. It is also likely that he sent requests to Venice and other parts of Italy, as well as Spain and possibly Austria, for the type of close-grained yew needed to make good bows. We can surmise that at least some of those that killed the French at Agincourt were made from imported wood.

Henry also attended to other aspects of the looming war. Just as the generals who commanded the Gulf War in 1991 spent months preparing and transporting material, so Henry expended time and effort in organizing the great engines of siege war that he knew he must take with him to France. Artillery, in the form of siege guns, was starting to play an increasingly important role in war. He also had

Henry V was a risk taker. After the siege of Harfleur he decided, against the opinion of his advisers, to march through the French countryside to Calais as a show of strength. He never intended to fight the French but when he met them on the open ground at Agincourt, the result was one of the most decisive moments in the history of warfare.

to find and pay private purveyors to deliver 'corn, bread, meal, or flour, wine, ale, or beer, fish, flesh, or any victuals, cloth, linen, woollen, or any merchandise, sheets, breeches, hose, shoes, or any other manner of armour, artillery, or any other stuff.' It was a vast operation.

He instigated a shipbuilding scheme – the royal fleet had dwindled to just a few ships – and within a few years he had vastly improved England's seafaring capabilites (he is sometimes cited as the father of the Royal Navy). He also seized any foreign ships berthed on the English coast. Dutch, Venetian and Genoese vessels were part of the flotilla that set sail from Southampton for France.

Contemporary chroniclers estimated that 1500 ships were used to transport 8000 archers and 2000 men-at-arms, plus baggage, siege guns, ladders, and food – and as many as 250 000 horses: *Trinité Royale,* the king's flagship, bearing all the requisite medieval glitter and glory – its top-castle was tipped with a crown of burnished copper-gilt and on the capstan was a sceptre wrought with the fleurs-de-lis – led the way. The day was 11 August 1415.

Unlike his immediate predecessors, John of Gaunt and the Black Prince, who embarked on a series of mobile operations through France which were successfully broken up by the harassing strategy of the French, Henry had decided to capture and secure a solid base from which he could strike deeper into French territory. John Keegan has noted that his thinking was not too dissimilar to that of the British and American strategists who planned the World War Two D-Day landings: Henry chose to set sail for the Normandy coast although it was anticipated that he would strike the coast at Bordeaux. His specific destination was the Bay of Seine and the port of Harfleur.

The siege of Harfleur is part of the crucial run-up to the battle at Agincourt. Henry landed his fleet unopposed on the coast, and marched to the well-fortified town. He set up camp nearby with all the material of an army away from home – tents and pavilions as well as subsidiary logistical support: carpenters, grooms and clerks, chaplains and surgeons, to name but a few. He then set about laying siege. He sent the Duke of Clarence to guard the other side of Harfleur to make sure no reinforcements marched into the town as well as to stop messengers from leaving it. Its gates were well protected with earthworks and moats and barbicans; so Henry's first impulse was to send men to dig mines under its walls in an attempt to destabilize them.

The French, however, were adept at digging counter-mines. As a result, Henry had to revert to a much more dangerous plan and call in the big guns. These were monstrous machines, lumbering and cumbersome by modern standards, but they were effective. Getting them into place cost the lives of many soldiers as the French had a clear shot at them from a number of Harfleur's 26 towers. Henry's men, grappling with ropes and pulleys in the August heat, were also easy targets for French men-at-arms who would dash out from the town in quick strikes and drag them back behind its walls.

But the true enemy was disease. Dysentery was taking its toll of the troops, striking archers, knights, earls and bishops indiscriminately. It was hot, flies buzzed around the latrines, the air was stagnant and the men ate mussels from muddy creeks which were, no doubt, amply fertilized by human and animal run-off. Medieval war was not known for its standards of hygiene.

The guns threw great gunstones, weighing up to 500 pounds (227 kilograms) at the walls and more ancient catapulting devices – the marngonal, ballista and trebuchet – added to the bombardment. However, the residents of Harfleur were spirited fighters, and although they never received any reinforcements they held off the attacks until mid-September when the guns began to take their toll. On 22 September they surrendered and handed the keys of the city over to Henry.

The English king had to make a decision. His initial plan to capture Harfleur and use it as a staging post for deeper strikes into French territory, possibly including Paris, had been a good one but the siege had lasted longer than he had expected. It was now late in the season and autumn rains and cold weather were descending. He felt he could not return to England because he would have fallen short of his declared intentions of taking territory and any later adventures in France would, as a result, be difficult both to promote and finance. He therefore decided on a risky, high-profile plan: a swift canter, or chevauchée, through French territory to Calais, his other stronghold.

According to English intelligence the French army was massing in Vernon, far enough away from Harfleur for Henry to calculate that his lightly equipped army could outpace it and reach Calais unopposed. The council of war, called on 5 October, listened with trepidation to the king's plan. His seasoned advisers cautioned him against it. But Henry replied with conviction:

> *Even if our enemies enlist the greatest armies, my trust is in God, and they shall not hurt my army nor myself. I will not allow them, puffed up with pride, to rejoice in misdeeds, nor unjustly, against God, to possess my goods … with the favour of God we will go unhurt and inviolate, and if they attempt to stop us, victorious and triumphant in all glory.*

The council of war could do nothing but give in.

Henry set off on 8 October with a diminished force – approximately 5000 archers and 1000 men-at-arms – on the 120 mile (190 kilometre) route to Calais. He crossed the River Béthune and then the Bresle without major incident, but as he approached the Somme – that river which snakes its way so painfully through British military history – he received some dire news. His advance guard had found and captured a lone Gascon who claimed to be the servant of Charles d'Albret, Constable of France, and one of Henry's enemies. He told the king that he could not ford the Somme at Blanchetaque, his pre-planned destination, because 6000 men were waiting for him under the command of Marshal Boucicaut.

After discussion with his advisers, Henry again rejected a retreat and decided to press south-east and follow the river inland. Five days passed as the French kept pace, shadowing the English from the north bank of the river. Henry's troops were close to despair. They were cold, tired and hungry – they had finished their rations and were living on nuts and dried meat – and the surrounding countryside had been cleared of anything that might benefit them by way of food or booty. In addition, Henry had all his troops on the strictest of behaviour. No looting or pillage was allowed; a man caught stealing from a church a few days earlier had been hanged and the entire army forced to march past his dangling corpse.

The army across the river had been steadily building in number and was now rumoured to be 100 000 men. On the sixth day, geography came to Henry's aid. There was a big bend in the Somme and by leaving its bank and cutting across the chalk downland of the Santerre, he stole a day's march on the French. They had to follow the bank up and around – in a sense covering two sides of a triangle – while the English cut across in a straight line. With the aid of some peasants, Henry discovered crossings at Béthencourt and Voyennes and hastily got his men across the Somme.

THE BATTLE

ONCE HENRY HAD CROSSED the Somme he was, in effect, on a collision course with the opposing army. On the following day, 20 October, French heralds found the English and announced that they were going to challenge Henry in the field. Neither Charles VI nor his son, the dauphin, were commanding the French forces – that was left to the dukes of Orleans and Bourbon and Constable d'Albret. Henry ignored this stately and formal request and declared that he was marching on; the French could find him wherever he happened to be.

Henry was pushed for both time and space and he decided to forge ahead with speed. He marched his army 18 miles (29 kilometres) on 21 October, and another 53 miles (85 kilometres) during the next three days. During the course of these marches the French, who had been close by but out of sight, crossed the path ahead of the English. The footprints and wheel tracks they left in the mud were terrifying evidence of the size and strength of their army.

The *Gesta Henrici Quinti*, The Deeds of Henry V, is a firsthand account of these marches, and of the battle of Agincourt, probably written by Thomas Elmham, the king's chaplain. Even through the formal, religious language of the time the despair at this juncture, just before the battle, is clearly apparent:

> ... we found, about a mile away, the roads quite remarkably churned up by the French army as it had crossed ahead of us many thousands strong. And the rest of us in the army (for I will say nothing of those in command), fearing battle to be imminent, raised our hearts and eyes to heaven, crying out, with voices expressing our innermost thoughts, that God would have pity on us and, of His ineffable goodness, turn away from us the violence of the French.

On 24 October the English caught sight of the French deploying for battle. They filled 'a very broad field like a countless swarm of locusts.' The armies manoeuvred inconclusively in the field; it was too late in the afternoon to engage in battle, so both sides bedded down for the night. The English settled into the small village of Maisoncelles, ate what little food they had and attended Mass. Henry was a religious man and when Sir Walter Hungerford said he wished that the king had 10 000 more archers under his command, he answered that, 'This people is God's people; he has entrusted them to me today and he can bring down the pride of these Frenchmen who boast of their numbers and strength.'

The English camp was quiet: weapons were checked, and some were repaired, archers waxed their strings and checked the feathered fletchings on their arrows, soldiers confessed to overworked priests and the battle-hardened veterans calmed the younger and more jittery of the troops. Henry urged his troops to sleep – they had marched for 17 days with only one day's rest and had covered over 250 miles (400 kilometres) and needed as much revitalizing rest as they could manage. Lieutenant-Colonel A.H. Burne describes how their camp was so silent that French outposts thought the English were preparing to slip away under cover of darkness. Some time in the early hours rain began to fall.

The French camp was the total opposite. The noise it made was a vast hum in the night. Men shouted to each other, clashed their armour and marched the horses up and down in front of the camp – a foolish move as the next day their soldiers were to charge over what was now muddy and uneven ground. They even threw dice through the night to decide who would capture Henry; the English archers were seen to be so worthless that they were counted as blanks. One chronicler describes how the French painted a cart in which to promenade the king through the streets of Paris.

Henry V. When he came to the throne he was in a politically vulnerable position. His father, Henry IV, had seized the crown from Richard II and years of political turmoil ensued. Henry V ascended the throne in 1413. As an astute leader he knew that victory abroad in France would help smooth over any problems at home.

The morning of 25 October 1415 broke cold and wet. Henry rose at dawn and heard Mass. He wore the royal surcoat decorated with the three leopards of England and the three gold fleur-de-lis of France. Bravely, he placed his impressively bejewelled crown on top of his basinet helmet. He was clearly marking himself out as target.

The ratio of English to French troops was staggering. Henry had between 5750 and 6000 men and the French 25 000 or even more – as many as 60 000 according to some sources. The two armies took up their positions at either end of a long and relatively flat stretch of field which had recently been sown with wheat. The width at the French end was about 1200 yards (1000 metres) while at the English end it was much narrower. At the point where the two armies were to meet it was approximately 900 yards (820 metres). From the English point of view, the village of Agincourt was on the left, behind a clump of trees, and Tramecourt on the right. The road to Calais stretched dead ahead, with the rolling mass of the French army blocking the way.

Accounts differ, but the two sides were separated by about 1320 yards (1200 metres) and clearly visible to each other. The rain had lifted and the autumn sun was low in the sky, behind the English and shining straight into the eyes of the French. The English men-at-arms took up battle positions in three blocks, standing only about four deep: it was a line, in the military sense, but it was a thin one. Henry was in the centre block, the Duke of York to the right and Lord Camoys to the left.

The role and exact placement of the archers in the battle formation has recently been the subject of heated debate. Robert Hardy, the actor and historian, is the proponent of the view that they were positioned on the flanks but that they were also arrayed next to the men-at-arms in wedge-shaped groups. He has the backing of a great deal of previous scholarship built on first-hand testimonies. Matthew Bennett, on the other hand, argues that this view is based on a misreading of one of these texts and, more specifically, a mistranslation of one word: *cuneos*. Instead of translating it as 'wedge', he believes that there is another interpretation and favours a broader definition as 'troop or unit'. He argues that although there were some archers towards the middle of the formation they were deployed in mobile, roving units, and contends that the clear majority of archers were on the flanks. This is more than pointless military minutiae; the archers were crucial to England's victory at Agincourt and their stance and position on the battlefield throws light on what actually happened.

The French were drawn up in three large lines. The first two 'battles', or groups of soldiers, were made up of 8000 dismounted men-at-arms packed in at about eight men deep. Towards the rear was a smaller group of crossbowmen, archers and some artillery; neither contributed significantly to the actual fighting. Behind them, in a third 'battle' was a large group of mounted men-at-arms. These groupings were stacked one behind the other, while those of the English were in one line. Cavalry divisions flanked the first French battle; they were positioned to swoop down on the archers on the English flanks. On both sides proud men of rank such as knights and nobles flew their armorial banners. On the French side noblemen tussled and shoved to get into the first division, and so have pride of place. Eighteen of them had sworn to each other that their sole intention was to kill or capture Henry and that they would fight to the death to accomplish their mission.

In the early hours Henry mounted his small, grey horse and rode up and down among his men. Dressed in his battle gear, with his sword held in his hand, he addressed his troops in 'a loud, clear voice'. He reminded them that he had brought them to France to recover his lawful inheritance and that he had good cause to claim it. In other words, this was a just war. He urged his troops to strive in battle so that they could return to their families with great glory and fame, and reminded them that previous kings of England had won noble victories over the French. He also repeated a rumour that the French were planning to cut three fingers from the right hands of the archers they captured so that they would never shoot again. Although it is next to impossible to verify this, its effect on the troops can be imagined. The anger and insult roll through the ages: the 'two-fingered salute', the archer-influenced equivalent of the middle-fingered 'up yours' is a British gestural legacy. It says: 'Just you come and try it, mate.'

Some ineffectual negotiations took place over the next 3 or 4 hours. For the soldiers, drawn up and ready for battle, the waiting must have been extremely trying. It was cold and wet and John Keegan has noted that many of the Englishmen were suffering from diarrhoea. Because they were deployed and ready for action, they would not have been allowed to break ranks and relieve themselves. The squalor, especially for the men-at-arms locked into all-enveloping armour, hardly bears thinking about. Medieval war was a messy business.

At about eleven o'clock, Dafydd ap Llewellyn, a Welsh captain who had been taking a closer look at the French army, rode up to the king who asked him to estimate the number and strength of the enemy. Llewellyn replied, 'Sire, there be enough to be slain, enough to be taken, and enough to be chivvied away.' Spirits lifted as this report circulated through the troops and Henry took advantage of this upsurge in morale; he knew that the French were not going to be drawn into an attack and that he had to make the first move. The order went out to advance.

The English covered some 700 yards (640 metres) of muddy ground in about 10 minutes. This was not a charge, but a slow and relatively orderly advance. The army probably stopped a few times for the men-at-arms, each weighed down by approximately 80 pounds (36 kilograms) of armour to catch their breath. When the troops reached a point that was approximately 250-300 yards (230-270 metres) from the French they stopped.

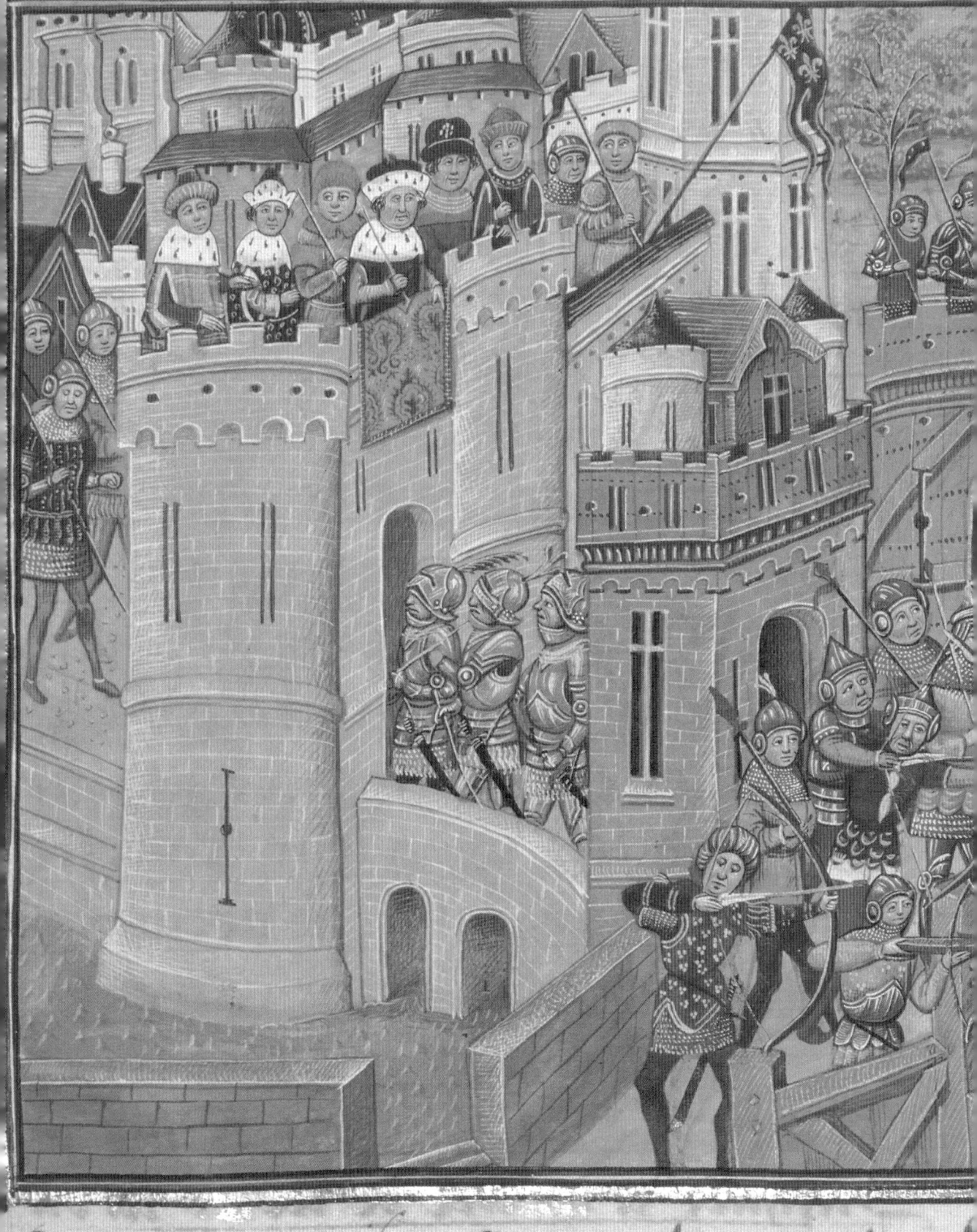

Er fait mention coment les anclois

uszent escarmuchier au belleberg

At the suggestion of the Duke of York, the archers had been carrying long stakes, sharpened at both ends, since the tenth day of the march when they had an inkling that the French cavalry would attack them. The historian Jim Bradbury suggests that this was not a novel technique. Novel or not, the archers had gamely carried the stakes for the rest of the march, and they now took them out on to the battlefield and planted them in the ground. Possibly with their backs to the enemy, they pounded them deep into the soil. It seems likely that the stakes were spaced at intervals, and slightly staggered so that although they were a fearsome threat to charging horses, they were not so tightly bunched as to impede the movement of the archers. The bowmen were probably about a yard apart, in 'chequerboard' formation which gave them a relatively clear line of sight that allowed them to shoot over the heads of their fellow archers. They were probably standing six or seven rows deep. Each man would have carried a sheaf, or possibly two sheaves, of 24 arrows.

Before the English advance the French had been building fires and eating breakfast. But they were now in a heightened battle-state. Oman refers, poetically, to a shiver passing through their line; this was the movement of the lances coming down into place, ready for attack. The prime function of the English archers was to provoke the enemy into such an attack.

The French cavalry was on the flanks, positioned to charge at the majority of the archers who had to group their arrows into a very narrow shooting zone and time their shooting so that its impact would be simultaneous and overwhelming. The shooting was indirect; the trajectory was steeply angled but the result was a distinct 'killing-zone' about 200 yards (180 metres) deep. It is not certain how the shooting was timed and co-ordinated, but it seems likely that there was a system of vocal signals. In this command and control model, 20 men would have been grouped under a 'vintenar' and five groups of 20 combined under a 'centenar'.

Clouds of English arrows soared into the sky, probably to a height of 100 feet (30 metres). One French chronicler wrote that it was as if they were hail and that they obscured the sky, another that they were like a thick fog and a third that they were like a snowstorm. The first salvo struck the men-at-arms waiting on the French lines. Their armour was deliberately designed to deflect arrows and their wide-brimmed helmets, or basinets, channelled the arrows away from their heads. Netheretheless, this first arrow cloud must have caused some significant damage; recent tests with contemporary approximations of the longbows found on the Tudor warship, the *Mary Rose*, indicate that arrows shot from a longbow have

PREVIOUS SPREAD: A medieval siege. Note the longbows and crossbows. A trained archer can shoot approximately sixteen arrows a minute to a crossbowman's two bolts per minute. During the long siege of Harfleur, Henry's army suffered more from dysentery than from the crossbows of the defending French.

penetrative power at up to 300 yards. But, as Keegan has noted, the primary goal of these first arrow clouds was not to kill; rather it was to provoke the enemy into a charge. The sound of the arrows falling on the bowed heads of the French must have been tremendous: a huge dissonant symphony as the bodkin-pointed weapons struck steel at high velocity. Mixed in with this roar was probably the sound of horses in extreme pain: the arrows would easily have penetrated their thick protective padding.

The burst of arrows had the intended effect; it goaded the French cavalry into a charge. Less than the anticipated number of horsemen joined in. Burne believes that as few as 150 out of the intended 600 on each flank actually took part. As they made their way across the muddy field towards the two main flanks of archers they picked up speed, as they were trained to do. Spurred on by their riders, the horses bore down hard on the archers, who probably shot another round of arrows. In the estimated 1½ minutes it took the French to reach the English line between 25 000 and 50 000 shafts were loosed at them. The archers were standing in front of the thicket of stakes and probably fell back only when the horses were almost upon them. St Rémy, a French chronicler who took part in the battle, states that, before their horses were impaled on the stakes, at least three French men-at-arms got in among the archers – who killed them as they fell to the ground.

The rest of the cavalry turned tail and galloped back into their now advancing line of dismounted men-at-arms. St Rémy's version is as follows: 'The greater part of them [the cavalry], with all their horses, from fear of the arrows, retreated into the French advanced-guard in which they caused great confusion, breaking and exposing it in many places ... their horses were so wounded by the arrows that they were unmanageable.' In 1919 James Hamilton Wylie wrote that the horses got 'haunched' on the stakes and 'flounced and plunged and would not face the buzzing arrows, but turned tail and galloped back in plumps, tearing huge gaps in the vanguard ranks'.

Because the dismounted men-at-arms were moving forward *en masse* it was difficult for them to open up gaps in their ranks to let the terrified horses and their riders through. The men-at-arms staggered and clutched each other, sending a violent ripple through the ranks. Keegan has made a brilliant analogy with what happened in the Grosvenor Square demonstration against the Vietman War in 1968 when a police horse, frightened by the demonstrators, charged into a line of policemen who reacted much as the charging French men-at-arms must have done: they held on to each other for dear life, and the surge and press that resulted brought many of them to the ground in a rippling, swaying scrum of bodies.

The French advance stalled and slowed, but it still came on. The men-at-arms were now much closer to the archers who were probably shooting straight into their ranks. Well-trained bowmen – and these men were certainly well trained – could shoot an arrow about every five seconds and sheets of arrows, shot by the

5000 archers, were tearing into the French. At this distance, they would have been able to pierce armour – an arrow can drive through an inch of oak.

The English archers had not entirely stopped the advance, but they had successfully channelled it into a narrower front of attack. At this stage French social convention came into play: the men-at-arms believed it was beneath their dignity to do battle with the socially inferior archers and, instead of attacking them on the flanks, or in the wedges between the 'battles' (according to Hardy's version), they pushed on towards the English men-at-arms, their social equals.

The French charge should not be underestimated. Despite the devastation wreaked by the archers, they were still a powerful and massive force. The English line of men-at-arms staggered as the two forces met but managed to hold their line. In fact, as they stepped backwards under the onslaught they effectively wrong-footed the French, who were pushing foward relentlessly, their lances aimed for attack – and whose numbers were now to their disadvantage as the steadily advancing men at the back pressed those in the front forward. The English were able to strike at them as they floundered. All the chroniclers agree that the press in the French lines was so tight that the men could hardly lift their weapons, let alone dodge or retreat, or side-step the blows that were raining down on them. The English men-at-arms could stab at them with impunity. At the same time, the archers were probably shooting their remaining arrows into the mass of the enemy. Within seconds, French bodies were piling up and the French column was effectively boxed in by them and by the press of solidiers from the back. Some men fell over in the crowd and suffocated in their armour as more bodies piled on top of them.

The success of the English longbowmen in provoking the French into a charge, and their ability to disrupt the charge and force the cavalry to ride back into their own ranks, was crucial in shifting the balance of the battle in favour of the English. '... it was arrows, not mud, that turned back the French horsemen and started the rot,' wrote Burne.

The longbowmen played yet another crucial role in the battle. As the French floundered and died at the hands of the English men-at-arms, the archers started to run out of arrows, and it is likely that the boxed-in French were beginning to contemplate a charge at these scantily protected men: archers wore very little armour, nothing more than a breastplate and small iron or wicker hat; some were even bare-legged. It was at this moment that the archers moved to the attack. St Rémy left the following account: 'The English archers, perceiving this disorder of the advanced-guard, quitted their stakes, threw their bows and arrows on the ground and seizing their swords, axes and other weapons, sallied out upon them ...'

One bowman was no match for a French man-at-arms, however tired, winded or disorientated, and it seems likely that the archers surged forth in small groups, picking off isolated soldiers as they found them on the field. While one archer stabbed at the slit in the enemy's visor, or into his face if he was wearing a basinet, another would send him sprawling with a well-aimed axe-stroke behind the knees. Keegan notes that each act of execution would have been swift and very violent, taking not more than a few seconds.

As the archers made concerted runs at the stalled men-at-arms, who were still pressing forward into the centre of the English line, panic started to set in among the French. As the French soldiers at the flanks started to retreat they opened up new areas within their ranks that were unaware of the archers' activity to their sides. These men must have been stunned when they were blind-sided by the charging bowmen. All this may have happened in as little as half an hour.

The English had broken the advance battalion and were making headway into

Although historically inaccurate, this picture is wonderfully evocative. Note the arrow in the horse. The first English arrow cloud at Agincourt goaded the French cavalry into attack and although many of those arrows did not initially disable the French knights they wounded the minimally protected horses. The significant thrust of the French attack, however, came from dismounted French knights.

the great mass of soldiers behind. Henry, clearly identifiable on the battlefield, was engaged in hand-to-hand fighting. His brother, Humphrey, Duke of Gloucester was felled by a dagger wound to his bowels; Henry stood over him, fought off his attackers, and so saved his life. None of the 18 French knights who had sworn to kill the English king succeeded, but one of them, the Duke of Alençon, got close enough to land a powerful blow on his helmet. One of the fleurons on his crown was reportedly sheared off. The attack was repelled and, according to one account, the duke surrendered to Henry but a loyal English soldier, thinking that he was attacking his king, ran him through with his sword.

The English had won. The wounded, the near-dying and the dead lay in heaps and the archers continued to kill the French, patrolling the writhing piles and administering quick, savage blows. According to battle mythology dead bodies were piled 6 feet (1.8 metres) high; it is more likely that they consisted of two or three layers of men. The newly sown field of wheat had become the site of a killing-field of almost unimaginable horror.

However, the fight was not yet over. Henry was aware that there was a formidable mass of mounted French soldiers in the distance who seemed to be preparing to strike. His baggage train to the rear had been attacked and he had lost some equipment and royal jewels. He had to make a difficult decision. His men had collected a large group of French soldiers who had taken off their helmets as a sign of their prisoner status and were standing towards the rear. If the mounted French attacked, his attention and that of his army would be divided, and it was possible that the prisoners would be able to break loose from the few men who were guarding them and attack from the rear. Henry therefore made the controversial decison to kill the prisoners. Many of his men-at-arms refused to follow his orders. One reason was that prisoners meant ransom, and money gained in this way was one of the traditional spoils of war. But there may have been a deeper reason for their reluctance: the chivalric codes of war. If you were a knight, fighting your social equal on a battlefield was the defining moment of your existence and defeating him was a crowning triumph. As Keegan has noted, there was no honour to be gained from killing your unarmed social equal, especially when he was your prisoner and, in a sense, your responsibility. Rather, it was a first step on the path towards dishonour.

A loyal band of 200 archers, led by an esquire, took care of the butchery, moving swiftly among the captives and killing them. We do not know how many men died, but we can be sure that it was a grisly sight. The prisoners who survived (mainly those for whom the highest ransoms would be paid) must have been shocked and terrorized – and, in effect, rendered harmless.

When Henry saw that the third French battle was not going to charge he stopped the massacre. It was mid-afternoon. His men spread through the battlefield, looking for more prisoners and stripping armour off the dead. As the author of *Gesta Henrici Quinti* wrote, the French, 'abandoned to us that field of blood together with their wagons and other baggage-carts, many of these loaded with provisions and missiles, spears and bows'. Also abandoned were approximately 6000 dead French soldiers – the English had lost about 300 men – who were buried by local peasants in pits on the battlefield.

THE WEAPON

THE MEDIEVAL LONGBOW is an elegant and simple device. Its simplicity is in its form: a stave of wood, cut from the trunk of a tree and strung with a piece of hemp.

The longbow used at Agincourt was about 6 feet (1.8 metres) long. The stave tapered somewhat at the ends, which were tipped with horn, and the bow was strung with a hemp or linen string cut to the requisite length – usually 11½ inches (34 centimetres) shorter than the stave. The string looped through the grooves in the horn tips causing the stave to bow about 6 inches (15 centimetres) away from the string. This is the classic and elegant curved profile of the longbow.

Its essential physics are also clear and wonderfully simple: it is, in essence, a two-armed spring spanned by a string. When the arrow, usually made of ash or poplar, is properly positioned and the string is drawn, the bow stores potential energy. On release, this energy is transferred to the arrow which is thrown into flight; in more scientific language, the elastic energy of the bowstave is transferred to the kinetic energy of the arrow. As the physicist Gareth Rees points out, the longbow is only slightly less efficient than an ideal spring. The energy stored in the bow, called the potential energy, is dependent on the force needed to pull back the bowstring. This is called the draw weight.

During the process of drawing back the bow, tensile stress increases on its back or outside, while at the same time compressive forces develop on its belly or inside curve. The ideal bow should be able to withstand these pressures without breaking. The choice and seasoning of the wood is crucial. Black walnut, hazel, ash, red mulberry and common elm have all been used to make longbows; but the ideal wood, by far, is the light, springy but strong wood of the yew tree (osage is a close second).

Yew is a mythical and powerful wood, from a sacred tree. A writ issued to Nicholas Frost, Henry V's principal bowyer, just before the Agincourt campaign requires him not only to find workmen to make and repair the king's bows but also to gather as much yew wood for them as he could find. But he explicitly forbade him gathering wood from ecclesiastical land. Yew trees, dark and formidable and strangely haunting, are often found near churches, probably reflecting an older, pagan tradition that early Christians incorporated in their worship.

THE LONGBOW

It took a draw power of 150-170 pounds to work a longbow. It takes huge strength, stamina and years of training to be able to manage this

Despite being tired, hungry, wet, a long way from home, and facing a French army many times larger – the English army placed its trust in its archers. Their job would be to neutralize the French cavalry

Unlike the men at arms, the archer had limited protection – and no armour. Even if it had not impeded him, few archers would have been able to afford armour in any case

Coming from all over England, the archers were yeomen – farmers, butchers, carpenters and people from the middle ranks of British society. Their French opponents were landed noblemen, and considered the archers as little more than peasants

Archers in Henry's army could be as young as 12 years old. The majority were in their late teens and early twenties

A good archer could fire as many as 15 arrows per minute, and with deadly accuracy

Two-handed broadsword

Defensive stakes, driven into the ground, at 45 degree angles and sharpened to protect the English against a charge of horses

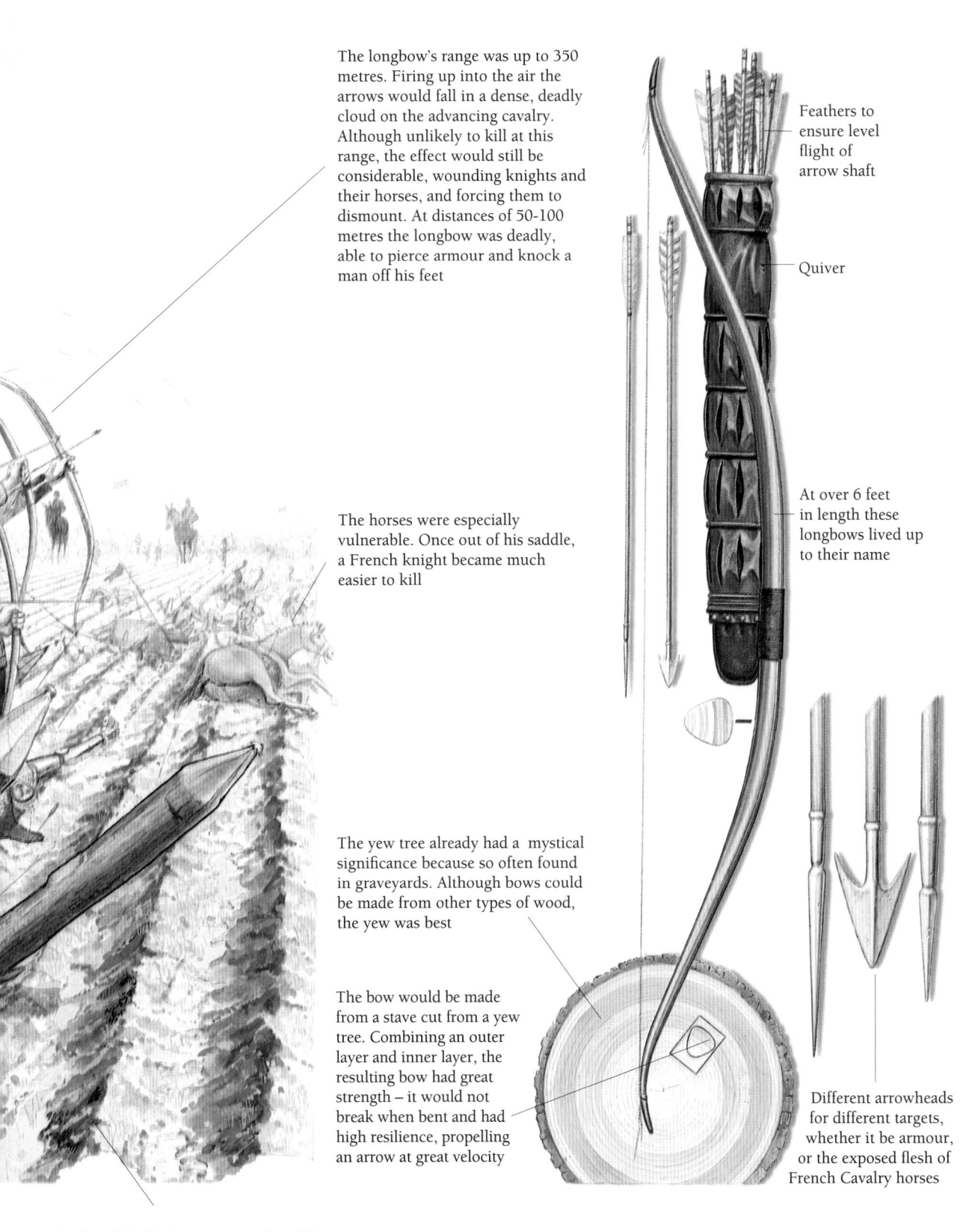

The longbow's range was up to 350 metres. Firing up into the air the arrows would fall in a dense, deadly cloud on the advancing cavalry. Although unlikely to kill at this range, the effect would still be considerable, wounding knights and their horses, and forcing them to dismount. At distances of 50-100 metres the longbow was deadly, able to pierce armour and knock a man off his feet

The horses were especially vulnerable. Once out of his saddle, a French knight became much easier to kill

The yew tree already had a mystical significance because so often found in graveyards. Although bows could be made from other types of wood, the yew was best

The bow would be made from a stave cut from a yew tree. Combining an outer layer and inner layer, the resulting bow had great strength – it would not break when bent and had high resilience, propelling an arrow at great velocity

The day of the battle was wet and muddy, further impeding the French horses

Feathers to ensure level flight of arrow shaft

Quiver

At over 6 feet in length these longbows lived up to their name

Different arrowheads for different targets, whether it be armour, or the exposed flesh of French Cavalry horses

When correctly cut the wood in the yew acts as a natural composite: the sapwood and the heartwood lie next to each other and a skilled bowyer will cut the stave accordingly. After the wood has been cut and then dried for a few years it provides the basis for an extremely accurate, sturdy and deadly weapon. In the Middle Ages, when there was a great demand for the wood, much attention was given to the growth of the trees. They were pruned of suckers, off-shoots and anything that limited straight growth. The wood was the raw material of the medieval armament and was protected and tended with all the care and diligence that we lavish today on the ingredients of our nuclear arsenals.

However, finding the ideal yew tree is difficult. English wood improves the further north you go – Scottish yew is better than English. Welsh yew is also useful if the tree grows on high ground but some of the best yew is found in Spain, Austria and northern Italy. There was a sophisticated European trading network in yew wood in medieval times and some of the bows used at Agincourt were made from non-English wood as a result.

Arrows were usually made from ash or poplar wood. Two or three feathers were placed at the nock, or blunt end, to stabilize flight – a law required that six feathers from every goose killed in the land be handed in for arrow fletching – and the arrows were tipped with long bodkin heads. These were the product of what was sophisticated forging for the time: the steel was hardened at the tip in order to penetrate plate armour and chain mail but the shank was softer to limit shattering on impact and so increase the likelihood that the arrow would remain intact and deliver a nasty wound. Arrows were lethal weapons, carefully constructed to maximize their potential for damage. Some of the heads were dipped in beeswax not only to minimize the risk of rusting during storage but also to act as a lubricant when it encountered the friction of armour on impact.

The defence against arrows was armour. The effectiveness of the longbow meant that protection against it became increasingly sophisticated. As the threat grew the armour made a slow but steady transition from chain mail to plate. Recent tests have shown that armour functions by either absorbing or dissipating the energy of the arrow. When the angle of the arrow as it bears down on its target increases, the depth to which it penetrates the armour decreases. The first clouds of arrows launched at the French at Agincourt would have struck their targets at a steep angle. Although they would have caused physical damage this was not their sole point; the intention was to goad the French into an attack. When the archers shot at a flatter angle the devastation was more severe. Archers shooting accurate, contemporary approximations of the longbows used at Agincourt say that it is possible to aim at, and strike, the vulnerable joints of armour – at the throat, the armpit and the groin – from 50 feet (15 metres). The arrows could penetrate metal up to 1.5 millimetres thick and would have had the velocity and power to punch through breastplates and visors. But most of the damage to the French would have been to their arms and legs, thus effectively disabling them as a fighting force.

THE VERDICT

THE FRENCH MEN-AT-ARMS at Agincourt insisted on charging into the lethal shooting-zone of the English longbow. Their urge to 'close' in the time-honoured, man-to-man style of the chivalric code sealed their immediate fate. As Robert O'Connell has put it, the knight was the human equivalent of some over-specialized reptile. As the conditions of war changed, he was locked into a pattern of response which only exaggerated what had once made him invincible. His armour grew heavier and his mobility on the battlefield became slower.

The recent discovery of a French plan for attacking Henry V's army at Blanchetaque on the Somme also sheds light on the battle at Agincourt. The French military planners were not inept; the plan for the Somme engagement details a very specific attack on the English archers by crossbowmen, a rear attack to cause confusion and an attack by cavalry and dismounted men-at-arms that would have been co-ordinated and effective. As Bennett has pointed out, the vestiges of this plan can be seen at Agincourt, but the huge increase in the size of the French army in the days between the possible encounter at the Somme and the battle made it ineffective. A divided chain of command, a poor choice of battlefield, a string of poor tactical and strategic choices and the power of traditional notions of chivalry also contributed to their defeat.

But it was the longbow's victory over the French knights at Agincourt that had a profound impact on the history of war. It undermined a basic Western prejudice against killing at a distance and contributed to a new ethic of fighting that would define modern war. Chance, impartial killing and anonymous death would all come to rule the battlefield of the future. Agincourt helped lay the foundations for what was to come later: bullets fired from machine-guns, strategic bombing and laser-guided missiles. These are technological escalations of Agincourt's decisive lesson: the importance of killing accurately from a distance.

The history of war is too often made abstract, a statistical and technical demonstration of killing ratios, specifications and tactical know-how. But war always comes down to the man on the field.

The last word on Agincourt belongs to one of the longbow men who actually fought there. Thomas Hostell, an archer who was wounded at Harfleur and Agincourt. He petitioned Henry VI as a result of being hit by a 'springbolt through the head, losing one eye, and his cheek bone being broken'. He was 'sore feebled and debruised, now fallen to great age and poverty, greatly indebted, and may not help himself ... being for his said services never yet recompensed nor rewarded.'

CHAPTER 2

THE BAYONET

'Twas for some time a dispute
between the swords and the bayonets; but
the bayonet was found by far the most
destructible weapon. The Regiment
behaved with uncommon resolution,
killing, some say, almost their
own number ...

CAPTAIN JAMES WOLFE,
ON THE BATTLE OF CULLODEN
(16 APRIL 1746)

THE CHALLENGE

ON 23 JULY 1745 a young aristocrat landed on the Isle of Eriskay off the west coast of Scotland after a dangerous and exhausting voyage. He had been at sea for 18 difficult days, during which his ship had been pursued by an English man-of war. He had evaded capture but his companion vessel had been forced to return to the French coast. On his arrival at Eriskay, he was met by representatives of the Scottish clans who informed him that their chieftains would not rise to aid him. But he was not dissuaded. On 25 July he crossed over to the Scottish mainland and in a series of intense discussions persuaded the reluctant clan leaders to support him. The young man's name was Prince Charles Edward Stuart, dubbed 'The Young Pretender'. He was to become the 'Bonnie Prince Charlie' of legend and would lead the Highland clans to unprecedented military successes but ultimately to destruction on the field of Culloden. There, the tribal warriors would be massacred by the regimented lines of the Duke of Cumberland's army, which had put its faith in a new drill with an old weapon: 17 inches (43 centimetres) of tempered steel called the bayonet.

An eloquent visual image neatly sums up the essence of the conflict at Culloden. William Hogarth's *The March to Finchley* shows the call-up of men in London as they prepare to march off to meet Charles Edward Stuart and his Highlanders. At first glance it looks straightforward: people lean out of windows watching the scene below, babies cry and a soldier in the foreground concentrates on his drum as he no doubt beats out a suitably martial tune. But the focal point of the engraving is a slightly removed tableau of three figures. A concerned soldier stands out from the crowd, staring into space. On his right a pregnant woman grasps his arm and looks intently up into his face. On his left a shrew-like woman attacks him; her hand, raised menacingly in the air, clutches an opposition newspaper. As the historian Linda Colley has perceptively pointed out in her landmark book, *Britons*, the image is much more than a depiction of men going off to war. It is a visual microcosm of a nation in crisis.

The soldier is Britain itself. The pregnant woman symbolizes the Protestant Hanoverian dynasty which was largely Protestant. The woman on the soldier's left represents the Stuarts and it is no mistake that a cross dangles conspicuously from her neck indicating that she is a Roman Catholic. Hogarth is, of course, prejudiced

PREVIOUS SPREAD: This picture sums up the whole battle as the English soldier plunges his bayonet in the targ of his enemy, a Scottish Highlander.

– there is no doubt that this is an English patriotic image. But the engraving makes a more general point: at this juncture in British history politics was deeply interwoven with questions of religion.

Charles Edward Stuart and his supporters stood for the restoration of the Roman Catholic dynasty that had been deposed in the 'Glorious Revolution' of 1688 when the prince's grandfather, James II, was forced to flee to France. The English crown had passed to Mary, his Protestant daughter, and her husband, William of Orange. William was both Dutch and Calvinist and therefore, in the eyes of a parliament determined to avoid the supposed evil of a Roman Catholic monarchy, a suitable king.

The 1745 rebellion led by Prince Charles was the latest – and last – of a number of attempts to restore the Stuarts to the throne. But 'the '45 was more a struggle for political expression by the Jacobite Highlanders who had suffered years of indignity since the ousting of James II than it was about religion. Nearly 70 years after the event, Parliament and the Protestant monarchy were still smarting from a Jacobite victory over William III's army at the pass of Killiecrankie in 1689. Nor could they forget that the Stuart dynasty was descended from the ancient kings of Scotland. James I, the first Stuart king of England, had been a Scottish monarch with all the characteristics of a Highland chieftain. It was politically adept for the Jacobites to harness the clansmen's loyalty to this historical past by linking it to a resurgence of the dynasty. It was in the British government's interest to stamp out this resurgence.

It did so with a policy of divide and rule, playing one clan off against another and feeding on the natural hatred that existed between the Lowland Scots and their wilder neighbours in the north as well as on the generations-old rivalry between the Campbells and MacDonalds. Perhaps the most graphic example was in 1692 when an entire branch of the MacDonald clan was eradicated by a force of Campbell clansmen in the Glencoe massacre. A seventeenth-century version of what has become known as 'ethnic cleansing', the killing was authorized by Sir John Dalrymple, joint secretary of state for Scotland and a Lowland Scot. The leaders of most clans had sworn a timely oath of loyalty to the new king, but MacDonald of Glencoe was late in doing so and it was officially decided to make an example of him. The orders for the massacre are signed top and bottom by King William himself, indicating that the monarch had read and understood them. The Campbells, who were blamed for the massacre, became the scapegoats for an act of governmental genocide.

The Stuart claim to the throne was effectively barred in 1701 with the Act of Settlement, which limited the passing of the crown to a Protestant – and established the Hanoverian claim to the succession. Anyone who was Roman Catholic, or married to a Roman Catholic, was 'forever uncapable to inherit, possess, or enjoy the crown and government of this realm'. The law is still valid today. In 1707 the Act of Union made England and Scotland one nation. In the memorable words of the pamphleteer and novelist Daniel Defoe, it was a union of policy, not of affection. In 1714 the Lutheran George Louis of Hanover became Britain's first Hanoverian monarch.

Resentment ran deep in the Highlands but an uprising in 1715, led by John Erskine, the 6th Earl of Mar, foundered even before James II's son, 'The Old Pretender' who had inspired it, had set foot on the shores of Scotland. An attempt to raise the Stuart flag again in 1719 was strangled at birth by disagreements between its commanders and firmly stamped out at Glenshiel. Neither uprising received the expected support from France or Spain – and the French actively tried to stop the pretender crossing the English Channel in 1715.

In 1745, therefore, clan leaders were understandably circumspect in their support of the Jacobite cause. Indeed, MacDonald of Boisdale, one of the first chieftains to meet Charles, advised him to go home. The prince replied: 'I am home sir, and I will entertain no notion whatsoever of returning to that place from whence I come; for I am persuaded that my Highlanders will stand by me.'

The chiefs may have been persuaded by this gutsy determination, or perhaps they had simply had enough of the discrimination which they had endured for so long. When the standard of rebellion was finally unfurled in the Highland valley of Glenfinnan on 19 August Charles was joined by MacDonald the Younger of Clanranald, MacDonald of Keppoch, MacDonnell of Scotus and the influential Donald Cameron of Lochiel. Even so, he had fewer than 1500 men. However, once the rebels had avoided a Hanoverian army twice their size and had marched into Edinburgh on 17 September that number had swelled to 2500.

The first battle of the '45 was on 21 September at Prestonpans on the Firth of Forth in south-east Scotland. Most of the Hanoverian army was in France and Germany and General Sir John Cope, the commander-in-chief of Scotland, was able to scrape together an army of only 2300 men which was made up of 2½ understrength battalions of infantry and two regiments of dragoons, plus six cannon. His troops were, on the whole, green recruits who had never been tested in battle and the cannon were manned by a team of inexperienced naval gunners. They were facing Highland clansmen practised in the arts of border warfare. The result was inevitable. The Hanoverian army was smashed, Cope was replaced and the number of Jacobite recruits drawn from both Highlanders and Lowlanders doubled almost overnight.

At the start of the uprising, as the Jacobites marched south through Scotland

PRINCE CHARLES EDWARD STUART (1720-1788)
Bonnie Prince Charlie was a dashing man and a source of inspiration for
the Jacobite cause. After his resounding defeat at Culloden, he escaped to
France and degenerated into a drunken shadow of his former self.

into England, the machinery that was in place to react to such an invasion worked poorly, if at all, and there was no over-all system of co-ordination for civil defence (the forces in the border town of Carlisle surrendered to Charles's army partly because no one had paid them for two months). Yet only 300 Englishmen joined the Jacobite cause. And almost all the major Scottish towns occupied by the Highlanders showed public as well as passive pro-Hanoverian sympathies. As Linda Colley has argued, this was probably a result of commercial and economic ties that the Scots had formed with the English after the 1707 Act of Union. They were not certain that a radical change in the dynasty was in their long-term interests.

This preference for the *status quo* began to affect the Jacobites. On 4 December when they entered Derby in central England less than 4500 men remained of the 5000 who had crossed the border just one month previously. The lack of public support for Charles Edward Stuart, combined with the rather more forthright support for the existing order in prosperous sectors of the civilian population, was a major factor in the decision – made against the wishes of the prince – to retreat from Derby rather than continue on to London.

Foremost among those who advocated caution was Lord George Murray, Charles's most astute military strategist. He had masterminded the defeat of Cope at Prestonpans, and foiled an attempt by William, Duke of Cumberland, to catch the dwindling Jacobite force as it retreated to the Highlands. But Murray's difference of opinion with the prince over Derby and his dislike of Colonel John O'Sullivan, one of Charles's closest advisers, created an irreconcilable gulf between him and the young pretender. In the months to come Charles would never wholly trust Murray's advice, believing that it was tainted with over-caution.

In Scotland the prince's army was reinforced by a token force of 800 Irish Piquets from France and six cannon. He celebrated his 25th birthday on 20 December 1745 and was pleased to see his ranks swell with Highland volunteers. On 17 January 1746 his army of 8000 foot and horse surprised a government force of roughly the same number under General Henry Hawley outside Falkirk in central Scotland. The resulting battle was inconclusive with the left flanks of both the Highlanders and the Hanoverians giving ground. But thanks to the timely intervention of Lord George Murray, who secured the high ground for the Jacobites, it was Hawley's men who were forced to abandon the field. Murray wrecked his chance of rehabilitation by complaining about the lack of discipline of the prince's beloved Highlanders. This, combined with his refusal to wait for dark before advancing on to the high ground as Charles had requested, did little to endear him to his sovereign.

Had Charles seized the opportunity to pursue the demoralized Hanoverians he could have landed a decisive blow. However, he listened to bad advice and settled down to a protracted siege of Stirling Castle instead of marching on Edinburgh, where the Hanoverians had retreated, as others had advocated. The result was disastrous. The clansmen, unsuited to the long-term demands of a drawn-out siege, began to drift away. The haemorrhage of manpower became so great that Lord George Murray was forced to present the prince with a written 'memorial' from himself and six clan chiefs demanding an immediate withdrawal into the Highlands to recruit more men and improve morale. Charles tried to argue against this but, as in Derby, he was overruled. It was another nail in the coffin of the relations between Charles and his best commander.

The Jacobite army withdrew to the Highland town of Inverness for the rest of the winter. But the Duke of Cumberland was not idle. In Aberdeen, 100 miles (160 kilometres) to the south, he introduced a new bayonet drill and trained his men to deal with the fearsome Highland charge.

THE BATTLE

ON 8 APRIL 1746 Cumberland felt ready to face the Jacobite Highlanders. His men were rested, well trained and had been reinforced by 5000 troops under Prince Frederick of Hesse-Cassel and several companies of the Argyll militia provided by Clan Campbell. He had about 9000 men, of which 2400 were cavalry, and his cannon were manned by members of the Royal Regiment of Artillery.

The duke marched north and sent a reconnaissance-in-force ahead of him under Major-General Humphrey Bland to secure the route. The first real engagement came when one of Bland's subordinates, Lieutenant Alexander Campbell, rashly decided to patrol the area around Strathbogie, half-way between Aberdeen and Inverness. He overextended himself and decided to spend the night in the small town of Keith where he was surprised by Lieutenant Nicholas Glasgow and a detachment of the Irish Piquets. Eighty of Campbell's men and about 20 horses were captured. The rebels were forewarned of the Hanoverian presence and had excellent intelligence of Cumberland's route of march and intentions. The duke was furious.

The news of the Hanoverian approach prompted another of the furiously acrimonious debates that had become the hallmark of the Jacobite High Command. Lord George Murray did not believe that the Highland army was strong enough to face Cumberland's troops and advocated retreat but the prince and O'Sullivan were determined to fight. They ordered Murray to find a suitable site for the engagement somewhere between Inverness and the enemy encampment at Nairn some 16 miles (26 kilometres) away.

The Jacobites had little choice but to give battle. Inverness was the hub of the

rebels' supply operation and contained not just ammunition and equipment but also all their oatmeal. This was the staple diet of the Highland army and there was too much of it simply to transport elsewhere; and to lose it would have been disastrous for the rebellion. Lord George Murray was reluctant to engage with the enemy. He seems to have at first tried to forestall an engagement by choosing ground that was unsuitable for a Highland charge and would have forced a Jacobite withdrawal. However, he was rightly overruled by O'Sullivan, who selected instead an open expanse of moorland to the south of Culloden House.

Murray was horrified and pointed out that such exposed terrain was perfect country for Hanoverian cavalry and artillery, but entirely unsuitable for the Jacobites' infantry army. Nevertheless, the prince and O'Sullivan were adamant that

THE MARCH TO FINCHLEY BY WILLIAM HOGARTH
This picture symbolically sums up one version of the battle of Culloden. The
Guardsman in the foreground is a symbol of Britain, the pregnant woman in white
represents the Hanoverian dynasty and the Stuarts are represented by the hag on his
left. This is Hogarth in his most graphic mode as political and social polemicist.

a battle should be fought there. Charles had lost patience with the defeatist talk of Murray and his supporters. He believed that if he had ignored their advice he would now be marching on London. Instead, he was defending a seemingly insignificant patch of Scottish heath. His faithful Highlanders had routed the Hanoverians before and they would do so again. They would fight at Culloden on 15 April.

Cumberland was of a different mind. The Jacobite army, shivering and hungry, waited for a whole day on the exposed ground of Culloden Moor for Cumberland's attack. It never came. Eventually, Lord Elcho was sent east with a scouting party to find out what was happening at the Hanoverian camp. He returned with the news that they were having a party. The duke's men were celebrating their commander's 25th birthday in the warm barracks at Nairn.

Lord George Murray now saw how the inevitable defeat he so dreaded could be turned into victory. He gave up his fruitless argument for a retreat and proposed a night march on the Hanoverian camp to surprise Cumberland's drunken soldiers as they slept off the effects of their celebrations. The plan had panache and appealed enormously to Charles, who decided to back it wholeheartedly.

It went wrong from the start. Murray planned to set off from Culloden by 8 p.m. but so many men had deserted in search of food that the march was delayed for an hour. Even then, there were hundreds of stragglers and the Highlanders' progress, over difficult country in the dead of night without adequate illumination because of the need for secrecy, soon degenerated into a shambles. As dawn broke on the morning of 16 April, Lord George Murray assessed the situation in the area of Kilravock Castle, half-way to Nairn. Only the lead column, one-third of the Jacobite army, was with him and he had no idea where the other two-thirds were to be found. There was no chance of reaching the Hanoverian encampment before reveille and any attack he mounted would be outnumbered by more than three to one. A less cautious man might have attacked anyway, hoping that the element of surprise would make up for the lack of men; but Murray had by now lost all faith in the entire campaign. He called a hasty council of war with his officers (including O'Sullivan) and obtained their agreement to withdraw to Culloden. Messengers were sent to inform the other two columns of this decision but missed them in the dark. The prince was profoundly shocked and dismayed when he heard the news. 'I am betrayed!' he said, 'What need I give orders, when my orders are disobeyed?' His patience with Lord George Murray had finally snapped.

The rebels straggled back to Culloden and collapsed, famished and exhausted, in a position some way to the west of the ground chosen by O'Sullivan. Many drifted off in search of food and others simply failed to find their way back to the moor. Murray estimated that the futile march had lost him almost 2000 men. Those that remained were in no fit state to fight a battle. No sooner had they closed their eyes to sleep than the alarm was raised: Cumberland's army was on the march.

The eventual site of the battle was, if anything, less suitable than the one originally selected by O'Sullivan. The Jacobite line was strung out between two dry-stone-walled enclosures which formed the parkland of Culloden House, and while the one on the right afforded some kind of protection for that flank of the army, the other, on the left, fell away to the north leaving the Highlanders' left flank dangerously exposed. Murray was also aware that the enclosure on the right was not as secure as it might seem: it would be possible for the Hanoverians to dismantle its walls and enter it to outflank the Jacobite right unseen. He wanted to tear the walls down but O'Sullivan overruled him. However, O'Sullivan was aware of the danger and suggested that Lord Gordon's Regiment, posted in reserve, be positioned inside the enclosure to guard against the threat. According to an eyewitness Murray would not hear of it.

Lord George Murray's men, called 'Athollmen', were posted on the right, the position of honour traditionally occupied by Clan MacDonald. There is some debate as to whether Murray had requested this but O'Sullivan's disingenuous report suggests that he had been given the right the day before but had no desire for it now:

> *Lord George comes up and tells Sullivan, who had the honour of being near the Prince, that he must change the order of battle, that his men had the Right yesterday. 'But My Lord,' says Sullivan, 'there was no battle yesterday, besides it is no time to change the order of battle in the enemy's presence.' … 'Gad sir!' says Lord George, swearing, 'It is very hard that my Regiment must have the Right two days running when it is he himself who would have it so absolutely.'*

There was no love lost between O'Sullivan and Murray and it is reasonable to suppose that Murray had requested the honour of leading the night march on Cumberland's camp, and that this had been translated by circumstance into the position of honour on the new battlefield. Whatever the truth, the MacDonalds were deeply offended, with important consequences later in the battle.

The area in front of the Jacobite lines – some 545-655 yards (500-600 metres) of uneven, marshy ground dotted with watery depressions – was wholly unsuitable for the Highland charge. Furthermore, Murray's Athollmen were faced by a U-shaped enclosure belonging to Leanach Farm which blocked off half their frontage from the Hanoverian lines and around which they would have to manoeuvre.

Cumberland's army was arranged in three short lines flanked by cavalry with two cannon placed between every regiment on the front line. The duke was well aware of the strategic potential of the dry-stone walls and had placed most of his cavalry on the left under General Hawley, with orders to break their way through the southern enclosures and work round the rebel flank. In the event, this outflanking manoeuvre played very little part in the outcome of the battle, largely thanks to Lord Gordon's reserves. The Hanoverian left was anchored on the Leanach enclosure where Barrell's 4th of Foot stood on the end of the line, supported on the right by Colonel Munro's Regiment, under the command of Colonel De Jean, and from behind by the regiment of Colonel Wolfe.

The battle opened with a cannonade, a viciously one-sided affair since O'Sullivan as quartermaster had failed to bring up fresh supplies of ammunition for the Jacobite guns. The Highlanders endured this bombardment for at least 15 minutes before being ordered to charge. This was only partly the fault of the prince, who had taken up a position to the rear in the centre of the Jacobite line. Twice he gave orders to charge, but Murray refused the first because the Jacobite line was not yet fully in position. The messenger carrying the second cut was decapitated by a cannonball and Murray eventually gave the order himself.

By this time the demoralized Highlanders were restless. They are generally depicted as throwing down their muskets and hurling themselves in an unco-ordinated mass against the Hanoverian line, but eyewitness accounts suggest a rather more organized, if undisciplined, approach. It seems that they formed into two or three wedges and charged, firing their muskets sporadically without waiting for the order to fire at point-blank range. Their progress over the moor was hindered by the pools of water and the uneven ground. Lochiel's men, who were to the left of Murray's Athollmen, were forced by the terrain to swerve right and they collided with Murray's Athollmen just as they were swerving left to avoid the Leanach enclosure. The result was a confused mass of men jostling together on a narrow front.

At close range, the Royal Artillery switched to grapeshot. It tore great swaths through the tightly packed ranks of the charging Highlanders – but still they came on. At 50 yards (45 metres), the redcoat infantry opened fire. A well-trained musketeer could get off three rounds in a minute: they fired two volleys before the Highlanders reached them. Given the closeness of the Jacobite ranks they were almost guaranteed a hit with every shot and entire lines of Highlanders fell. Even this could not halt their charge. In the words of Alexander Taylor of Cholmondley's Regiment: 'They came running upon our front line like troops of hungry wolves.'

The regiment that had the misfortune to bear the brunt of this frenzied assault was Barrell's 4th of Foot. Could its men withstand the onslaught or would they break like so many redcoats before them? Captain-Lieutenant Thomas Ashe-Lee of Wolfe's Regiment was positioned behind them and witnessed their clash with the Highlanders, as did Private Michael Hughes of Bligh's Regiment beside him:

Poor Barrell's Regiment were sorely pressed by those desperadoes and outflanked ... It was dreadful to see the enemies' swords circling in the air as they were raised, and no less to see the officers of the army, some cutting with their swords, others pushing with their spontoons, the sergeants running their halberds into the

WILLIAM, DUKE OF CUMBERLAND (1721-1765)

He was the third son of George II and from his earliest days was a keen and committed soldier. He led the English to victory at Culloden and earned the nickname Butcher Cumberland because of his harsh treatment of the Scots afterwards.

throats of the enemy, while the soldiers mutually defended each other and pierced the heart of his opponent, ramming their bayonets up to the socket.

This seems very much like Cumberland's newly developed bayonet drill in action. Before the battle, he had exhorted his troops: 'My brave boys, your toil will soon be at an end. Stand your ground against the broadsword and target. Parry the enemy in the manner you have been directed.'

They were doing just that. In the words of another eyewitness:

Now the left hand bayonet attacked the sword fronting his next right-hand man. He was then covered by the enemy's shield where open to his left, and the enemy's right open to him. This manner made an essential difference, staggered the enemy, who were not prepared to alter their way of fighting, and destroyed them in a manner rather to be conceived than told.

Nevertheless, the momentum of the Highlanders' charge smashed Barrell's regiment in half: 'Making a dreadful "huzzah!" and even crying "Run, you dogs!" they broke in between the Grenadiers of Barrell and Munro; but these had given their fire according to the general direction and then parried them with their screwed bayonets.'

The brunt of the attack was transferred to Munro's, but the charge had lost its impetus and the regiment was able to hold its ground as an anonymous corporal records: 'The front rank "charged" their bayonets breast high, and the centre and rear ranks kept up a continual firing … the Rebels designing to break or flank us but our fire was so hot, most of us having discharged nine shot each, that they were disappointed.'

At the same time Wolfe's Regiment moved forward on to the flank and opened up a murderous enfilading fire into the mass of Highlanders milling around the Leanach enclosure. The clansmen were trapped on three sides, under continuous fire and faced by a hedge of bayonets. The result was never in doubt. As Murray himself put it: 'Nothing could be done – all was lost.'

The area in which so many Highlanders lost their lives is now mournfully known as the Well of the Dead and is marked by gravestones bearing the names of all the clans that were decimated in the massacre. The survivors staggered from the killing-ground and were hounded off the field by Hawley's Dragoons who had finally managed to work their way round the Jacobites' right flank and break through Lord Gordon's Regiment in the chaos of the rout.

On the Jacobite left the MacDonalds had not even managed to get into contact with the enemy. It has been said that they refused to charge out of anger at being denied the position of honour on the right, but with their left exposed to the cavalry on their flank and the ground so bad, they were probably never able to mount a coherent attack. When the right wing broke they too fell back and were soon part of the general rout.

Charles tried desperately to stem the flood, but to no avail. His bodyguard eventually spirited him away under orders from O'Sullivan who, to his credit, stayed and tried to co-ordinate the retreat. The bayonet had won the day.

THE WEAPON

LEGEND HAS IT that on a lonely ridge in the Pyrenees sometime during the seventeenth century, a group of Basque musketeers was surprised and surrounded by a company of Spaniards. Desperate and out of ammunition, their chances looked slim until as a last resort one of them took out his *'bayonnette'* and rammed it into the muzzle of his musket to create an impromptu spear. His companions followed suit and together they beat off the assault from behind a hedge of makeshift pikes. The ridge is called 'La Bayonnette' to this day.

The origins of the bayonet are in fact shrouded in mystery. The most popular theory is that it developed from a type of dagger manufactured by the armourers of Bayonne in south-west France, whence it got its name. However, the earliest reference linking the *bayonette* to Bayonne dates from 1694 and *bayonniers* were known as early as 1611. They were crossbowmen and the bayonet may have evolved out of the short swords they were renowned for wearing.

Such an origin seems fitting since the subsequent history of the bayonet is inextricably linked to the weapon that replaced the crossbow: the gunpowder musket. Like the crossbow, the early musket was cumbersome and slow to reload, and commanders in the field were faced with the perennial problem of protecting valuable but vulnerable troops while they reloaded their weapons. For a long time, the answer was to integrate musketeers with pikemen, a system refined by that innovative genius Gustavus Adolphus, the Swedish king whose army had become the model for all European armies during the seventeenth century. But this put manpower at a premium, and as the effectiveness of musketry improved the pike became a military irrelevance.

The earliest form of bayonet was the 'plug' bayonet, a dagger with a hilt that was designed to be inserted into the muzzle of the musket. It was used in France as early as 1642 when a French officer described his men as being armed with: 'Bayonnettes with handles one foot long, and the blades of these bayonnettes were as long as the handles, the ends of which were adapted for putting into the barrels of their fusils to defend themselves once they had fired.'

The disadvantages of such a weapon are obvious. A musket could not be fired with a bayonet attached but in the seventeenth century its effective range was no more than 50 yards (45 metres). This meant that by the time it had been fired the enemy was already so close that there was no time to fix the bayonet.

The natural response was to design one which could be fitted to the musket by means of a socket that slotted round the muzzle. By 1720 the British army had adopted the standard Land Pattern socket bayonet, named after the weapon it was designed to complement: the Long Land flintlock musket, affectionately known as the 'Brown Bess'. It was a 17 inch (43 centimetre) sliver of tempered steel, ground to a shallow, triangular cross-section and attached to the muzzle of the musket by means of a circular socket, in which was cut an L-shaped groove designed to slot round the sight and hold the bayonet firmly in place. It allowed the musket to fire while it was attached and did not get jammed down the muzzle or work itself loose. However, at Prestonpans and Falkirk, it proved a dismal failure.

This was largely due to the fearsome Highland charge – a sophisticated and co-ordinated attack designed to intimidate the enemy and to hit him with the maximum possible force in the minimum allowable time. It worked best when the Highlanders had the advantage of the high ground.

Most clansmen were armed with a short musket or a pair of pistols. With these, they would advance quickly to point-blank range and fire one devastating shot before drawing their broadsword, the claymore, and charging home. In hand-to-hand combat, the claymore was more than a match for the unwieldy bayonet which the Highlanders could deftly fend off with a small, buckler-style shield called a targe (or target) that was strapped to his other arm. In his targe hand he held a dirk, a long-

The order and discipline of the British against the awe-inspiring and ferocious charge of the Highlanders.

THE BAYONET

With a bayonet attached, the musket could revert to being used as a pike. For 300 years the British infantry has continued to issue them and they were used in the Falklands War

Claymore sword

The bayonet is here attached with a socket rather than plugged into the musket opening. This allows it to be fired while the bayonet stays attached

The King's army were trained how to counter a Highland charge. Each man would stab at the Highlander to his side – under his shield, relying on the red-coat next to him to kill the Highlander attacking him. This required faith and iron-nerved discipline, but it worked

The bayonet became the chief weapon of the British infantry. It gave them huge confidence even when facing numerically superior forces. It played a crucial part in the British defeat of Napoleon at Waterloo, the Imperial Wars of the nineteenth century, trench warfare in the Great War and its effects were felt even into the Second World War. Its use was supposed to instil naked aggression into the raw recruit and it remains a part of British infantry drill to this day.

Although supposed to be mostly English, George's army actually contained large numbers of Scottish lowlanders. Some people even claim more Scots fought against Bonnie Prince Charlie than for him.

The most terrifying aspect of a Scottish army was the so-called Highland charge. With men running en masse, screaming and wielding sword and shield, more than one English army had been terrorized into fleeing

Even today's NATO rifle still has a bayonet

The Highland Scots, or Jacobites, were in rebellion to help win back the throne for the Catholic Stuarts, away from the Protestant Hanoverians. Bonnie Prince Charlie who could barely speak English (and only in a thick Italian accent) gave the English a bad scare, but having reached Derby, was forced to retreat back to Scotland

Clan tartan – these plaids were banned after Culloden as part of the systematic destruction of the Highland way of life

Shield

The length and ferocity of the British bayonet was psychologically terrifying. Shorter, more effective bayonets were rejected because they weren't intimidating enough

With both cannon and musket-fire from the side, many of the Highland casualties were inflicted before the vicious hand-to-hand fighting began

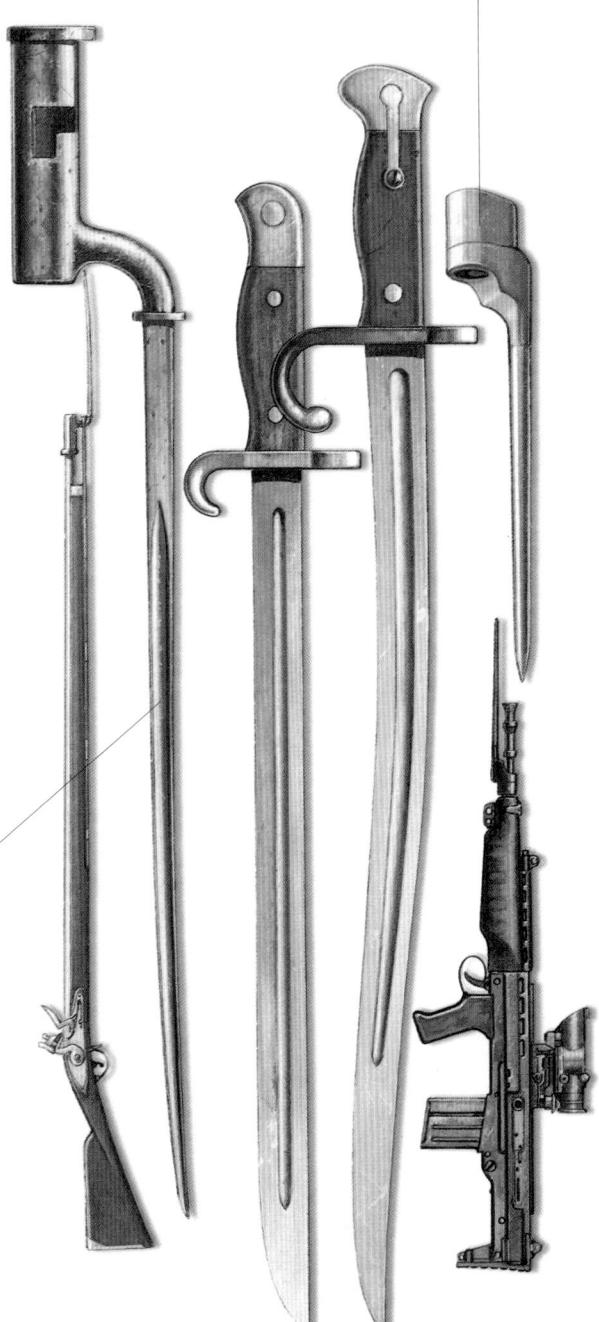

bladed dagger, with which he could riposte as he brought his claymore down in a classic overhead slash.

Used properly, the Highland charge was unstoppable. An eyewitness at the battle of Killiecrankie in 1689 said that the initial volley was fired at such close range that: 'It fired the beards of the enemy.' At Prestonpans and Falkirk, it brushed all opposition aside. Whether armed with plug or socket bayonets, the army inherited by the Duke of Cumberland after Falkirk seemed incapable of resisting the onslaught.

The duke was lucky to have unusually able junior officers, known as 'the Cumberland ring', under his command. Many went on to become successful generals in their own right while others went on to prominence in the colonies. The most famous was James Wolfe, later to earn schoolboy immortality by dying on the Heights of Abraham outside Quebec in Canada. In 1746 Wolfe was just 19 and witnessed events at Falkirk. His name appears with those of other junior officers on an after-action report that analyses how and why the Hanoverian army was defeated. Their conclusions are complex and must be viewed with the caution appropriate to a document that excuses a defeat, but they candidly admit that casualties on their left flank were so low because the infantry ran away rather than facing the Highlanders' charge. On the right, firm resolve and steady fire had kept the clansmen at bay.

The army was failing because its soldiers did not believe in themselves. As Wolfe put it:

> I have but a very mean opinion of the infantry in general. I know their discipline to be bad and their valour precarious. They are easily put into disorder and hard to recover out of it. They frequently kill their officers through fear, and murder one another in their confusion.

To give the infantry the confidence to face the Highland charge Cumberland and his staff developed a new bayonet drill. They went back to basics. The bayonet was designed to turn the musket into a pike so they trained the men to be pikemen. On the order 'Charge your bayonets!' the soldier raised his musket and held it level at shoulder height, grasping the butt end with his right hand, ready to push. This he did on the command 'Push your bayonets!' thrusting forwards with a shout. To this they added a refinement, supposedly suggested by officers of Barrell's 4th of Foot and based on an idea inspired by the Romans. The infantryman was trained to thrust his bayonet into the Highlander's exposed right side as the clansman, like Celtic warriors before him, raised his right arm to slash with his claymore. This had worked for the Roman legionary protected by his shield and it worked at Culloden.

THE VERDICT

THE REASONS FOR the clansmen's defeat at Culloden are still hotly debated. Some argue that the Highland charge failed because of broken ground and a lack of co-ordination that nullifed its usual frightening momentum. Others say that the Jacobite army had received terrible casualties from the artillery barrage beforehand and was further decimated by musket fire from both front and flanks. These arguments are valid, but the victors of the battle agreed unanimously that it was, above all, the bayonet that won the day. In his official report Cumberland stated: 'There was scarce a soldier or officer of Barrell's and that part of Munro's which engaged, who did not kill one or two man (sic) each with their bayonets and spontoons; not a bayonet but was bent or bloody and stained with blood to the muzzles of their muskets.'

The view of the majority of those who took part in Culloden is perhaps best expressed by a veteran of Barrell's 4th of Foot in a letter written after the battle: 'The old Tangereers bravely repulsed those boasters with dreadful slaughter, and convinced them that the broadsword and the target are unequal to the musket and the bayonet when in the hands of veterans who are determined to use them.'

The British army now had a faith in the combat effectiveness of the bayonet that it had not possessed before. The common soldier crowed that, 'The claymores could make no impression against the bayonet charged breast high.' The officers realized that, in the words of James Wolfe: 'Twas for some time a dispute between the swords and the bayonets; but the bayonet was found by far the most destructible weapon. The Regiment behaved with uncommon resolution, killing, some say, almost their own number …'

Born on the killing-grounds of Culloden, faith in the bayonet and its ability to stiffen the morale of troops was confirmed some 30 years later in the woodlands of New England where the Americans adopted it as their close-combat weapon of preference. It might be argued that the bayonet, as much as the Pennsylvania rifle, helped them to independence.

It was during the American Revolutionary War that the bayonet charge was perfected. Up to Culloden, bayonet drill had been a defensive adaptation of the antique pike-drill. The bayonet was the weapon of last resort with which the unloaded musketman received the charge of his opponent and tried to beat him back. Culloden showed Wolfe and his contemporaries – many of whom saw service as generals and governors during the American war – that it could be used to increase the aggression and resolve of fighting troops. The knowledge that the bayonet could defeat a murderous charge gave all ranks in the British army the confidence to advance while putting the fear of God into their opponents. In the woods of New England, on the Heights of Abraham, and in India the British soldier now had faith in the bayonet charge. Standard British practice in the colonies was to fire one volley before charging to contact the enemy – who generally retreated.

In India, where the army of the East India Company had been organized by Major-General Stringer Lawrence, a veteran of Culloden, the doctrine of British officers was to conduct lightning campaigns with a heavy reliance on the intimidating power of the bayonet. In this way, the 'thin red line' of the British army was able to intimidate forces that outnumbered it by as much as ten to one. One of these officers was a certain Arthur Wellesley, who was to take this doctrine and transfer it wholesale to the battlefields of Europe. Its success earned him fame and fortune as the 'Iron Duke' of Wellington.

The British military establishment viewed Wellesley with deep suspicion when he arrived on the Iberian Peninsula in 1808. 'European' thinking was very different to that practised in the colonies, whose graduates were seen as reckless 'sepoy generals'. This is best expressed in the British drill-book of 1788, which laid great emphasis on musket duels fought by the 'thick red line' – men arranged three deep to avoid the possibility of a bayonet attack. From this, it has been argued that the main advantage of the bayonet was that it allowed the concentration of massed firepower by a force confident that it could withstand any attack: with their bayonets fixed infantrymen could continue firing until the last possible moment.

Wellesley brought a new discipline to the Peninsular Wars: his infantry lined up behind the crest of a hill in a two-deep line and, as the French column of march crested the rise, surprised it with a single volley of musket fire followed by an immediate bayonet charge. On other occasions, he would thrust the British line forwards with express orders not to fire until the last minute and then to charge home. The list of battles won with these tactics is endless and includes those of Busaco and Vitoria, classics of their type, as well as Maida and San Christoval in which the mere sight of the bayonet was enough to see off the French – at Maida most of their casualties were stabbed in the back while trying to run away.

Throughout the Napoleonic Wars, from 1799 to 1815, the British army used the bayonet to win its battles. Even though the credit for the famous rout of the Old Guard – the imperial guard created by Napoleon – at Waterloo is generally given to Maitland's British Guards who rose from a concealed position and blasted them with musket fire, three of the five French battalions were repulsed by the bayonet charges of Halkett's and Adam's Brigades. By the end of the Napoleonic Wars the British army was so confident of its ability to defeat any enemy, that it could take on incredible odds and still come out victorious. The most famous example is the stand of the 93rd Highlanders against the Russian cavalry at Balaclava where the term 'thin red line' was coined.

The bayonet has become the emblem of the British infantry. It is on their badge and stands for all that is seen to be great about the army: its grit, its discipline and its iron determination. Even during this modern era of technological warfare, it has retained its mythic quality. Bayonets were fixed in 1917 before the men at Passchendaele went over the top to face enemy machine-guns, and they feature in propaganda photographs from El Alamein in 1942, where German tanks can be seen surrendering to the bayonet charge of British Tommies.

In 1982 members of Britain's Parachute Regiment fixed bayonets once again before their charge on Goose Green in the Falklands conflict. But these were pale, technological offspring of the ones used at Culloden. They were designed to act as tin-openers and wire-cutters rather than as weapons of war. Technology had moved on; killing was primarily a long-distance affair, achieved through a gun sight or a radar screen. But the role of the bayonet had not been entirely lost. One of its main purposes, in the Falklands as at Culloden, was to fire the morale of the troops and link them inextricably to the workings of the larger war machine.

BATTLE OF ALBUHERA (1811)
This battle was the classic example of the indecisiveness of firepower. After a forty-minute fire-fight, the French, who outnumbered the British three to one, were forced to withdraw. The French commander said, 'The day was mine but the British did not know it.'

CHAPTER 3

THE PANZER AND THE T-34

*The architect of victory is not the
infantry but the tank. If the tank fails, then so does
the whole attack. If the tank suceeds,
then victory must follow.*

HEINZ GUDERIAN,
THE GERMAN GENERAL WHO
INVENTED BLITZKRIEG

THE CHALLENGE

AT 4.45 A.M. ON 1 SEPTEMBER 1939 five German armies invaded Poland. Spearheads of armour and infantry thrust deep into the Polish heartland, outflanking the stunned army and bottling it up in isolated pockets that could be picked off at leisure. Within 27 days the invasion was complete, Poland had capitulated and the world was at war. It was the culmination of a cycle of treachery and appeasement that had reached its nadir with the infamous Munich agreement, which ceded the region of Sudetenland to Germany on 29 September 1938, and the invasion of Czechoslovakia in March 1939. The British prime minister Neville Chamberlain's celebrated 'piece of paper' that would secure 'peace in our time' had finally proven to be worthless and the world held its breath. The only question in anybody's mind was not 'whether' Germany would invade France, but 'when'.

The French High Command was confident that it could defend France against the blow when it came. The supreme commander of all Allied forces was General Maurice Gamelin, a career soldier who had served with distinction during the 1914-18 war and was now aged 68. He was convinced that Germany would invade through Belgium in a repeat of the Schlieffen plan of 1914. Drawn up by Field Marshal Alfred von Schlieffen in the years leading up to World War One, the plan envisaged the German army swinging through Belgium and northern France like a door slamming shut on Paris. Gamelin had established Plan D, otherwise known as the Dyle plan, to counter it. This assumed that it would take Germany nine days from the start of the invasion to reach a line formed by the Belgian rivers Dyle and Meuse. In that time the French army, and the tiny British Expeditionary Force (BEF) led by General Lord Gort, would push forward into Belgium to take up a defensive position along the Dyle–Meuse line and prevent the Germans from crossing. Gamelin's only worry was a space between the two rivers known as the Gembloux gap, and to this he had committed a mobile cavalry corps of two light tank divisions under the command of General R. Prioux.

The plan was a good one, given the political circumstances and the information available. The people of France still had painful memories of the last war fought on French soil, and their high command was determined that such devastation would not happen again. Therefore, the war would be fought in Belgium. However,

PREVIOUS SPREAD: With its sloping armour, rounded turret, and extra-wide tracks, the T-34 was ideally suited to countering the German advance on the vast plains of Russia. Simpler to drive than its German counterparts, and less prone to freezing, it spear-headed the Soviet Army all the way to Berlin.

it was not politically expedient to advance troops across the border until Germany had made the first move. In addition, captured German papers suggested that the German High Command (OKH), was considering a version of the Schlieffen plan for which the Dyle defence was perfectly suited.

The Allies were labouring under a misapprehension. They believed that they were going to fight a war similar to the last one and had not learned from the surprising collapse of Poland.

The Germans had learned. For them, Poland had been a giant experiment in a new kind of warfare, fought with new technology and requiring new techniques. They had made many mistakes there which they would not make again. When the assault on France came it would not be with the 'closing door' of Schlieffen, but with the *Sichelschnitt* (the cut of the sickle) of the blitzkrieg. And at the heart of the blitzkrieg would be the tank, given its baptism of fire during World War One but as yet uncredited with any decisive military achievement. In May 1940 that would all change, and it would be Germany's old enemy, the French, who would be on the receiving end.

THE BATTLE

OKH WAS LESS THAN HAPPY at the prospect of an invasion of France, and with reason. On paper, the French and their allies had one of the most formidable armies in the world: 144 divisions against 141 German ones; 13 974 artillery pieces against 7378; 3383 tanks against 2445. They also outnumbered the Germans in anti-tank capacity. On paper, the German army's only advantage was a significant superiority in air power.

Hitler wanted a swift thrust into France, realizing that the longer he delayed the more the situation favoured the Allies. However, OKH was not convinced that it could smash through the formidable looking French defences. Any attempt to attack France's eastern border, which directly abutted on Germany, was automatically doomed to failure because of the Maginot line. This warren of underground tunnels and gun emplacements was theoretically impregnable and had been designed specifically to deter any German attack. The only possibility was to go through Belgium. Yet that had been tried in 1914, and had ground to a halt on the French border in 1916 in the bloody morass that was the Somme. Hitler, however, was not interested in this kind of timidity, and the Germans took their gamble: the blitzkrieg would have to work; the panzer would deliver them a victory without succumbing to the stalemate of the Great War. That was what

Hitler wanted to hear and, reluctantly, the German army moved to give him what he wanted.

The first panzers to reach the Meuse were part of General Erwin Rommel's 7 Panzer Division, the advance elements of which arrived at Dinant on the afternoon of 12 May. Ever lucky, Rommel found that the scouts of his motor-cycle battalion had discovered a weir still intact at Houx and had crossed to form a precarious bridgehead on the west bank of the river. He now brought forward 'powerful artillery and tank support to deal with the enemy nests.' The tanks included the new PzKpfw IV. The assault began in earnest on the morning of 13 May. Captain Konig of the 25th Panzer Regiment remembers: 'The fire of the Panzer guns, the 75mm shells as well as the well-scattered 20mm quick-firing cannon soon show an effect ... The enemy fire begins to slacken noticeably, but nevertheless the crossing of the first storm boats, the engineers, remains a hard task ...'

The fighting was fierce and Rommel was everywhere, egging his men on to ever more desperate assaults. Slowly and painfully, the French units gave way. By the morning of 14 May 15 panzers were on the west bank of the Meuse. It was enough.

Further south, at the town of Sedan, General Heinz Guderian had somehow managed the impossible and threaded three panzer divisions through the needle-eye of the Ardennes. While Rommel had been advancing on the Meuse on 12 May, 1 Panzer Division had been battling its way towards the river against stiff resistance from 5 Division Légère Cuirassée (DLC), and by nightfall had forced it to evacuate the eastern half of Sedan. However, Guderian's artillery was still stuck in traffic jams in the Ardennes. By midday on 13 May he could wait no longer. His superior, General Paul von Kleist, ordered him to start the crossing at 1500 hours without the artillery and promised him full air support. There was so little time to issue the orders that Guderian's staff officers simply dusted off those used in training exercises for the Meuse crossing and altered the start times.

As well as 1 Panzer Division, Guderian had 2 Panzer and 10 Panzer Divisions at his disposal. Attached to 1 Panzer was the élite SS Grossdeutschland regiment, and in support was the full force of the Luftwaffe, which had dominated the air since the start of the campaign on 10 May. Against him were ranged only two 'B' class French reserve divisions, the 55th and the 71st, but these were dug into strong defensive positions overlooking Sedan on the Marfee heights. 1 Panzer and 10 Panzer were to assault the heights in a pincer movement around either side of the town. Meanwhile, 2 Panzer was to move further west and force a crossing at Donchery. This would bring it on to the west bank of the Meuse at a point where the 55th gave way to France's 102nd Fortress Division. However, its orders were not to support the attack on the Marfee heights, but to turn west and strike into the enemy rear areas. 2 Panzer was to spearhead the blitzkrieg.

True to von Kleist's word, at midday on the 13 May hundreds of Ju-87 Stukas came screaming out of the skies to bathe the bunkers of Sedan in an unprecedented storm of fire. Though the bombs were generally incapable of penetrating the deeper positions, these were repeatedly hit by flat trajectory shells fired from across the river by Guderian's panzers and anti-aircraft guns. Yet the 55th held, and when 10 Panzer's Pionere units brought forward their dinghies to cross the Meuse, they were met by a hail of fire from the heights. Grossdeutschland and 1 Panzer fared better. They managed to cross the river in the vicinity of Glaire village, west of Sedan, and fought their way doggedly on to Wadelincourt at the foot of the Marfee heights where they ground to a halt. They would have stayed there had it not been for one of those freak circumstances that often occur in war.

A French artillery officer near the village of Chaumont reported seeing some tanks which he thought were German up on the Marfee heights. The report was untrue – no German tanks had yet crossed the Meuse – yet like some malevolent Chinese whisper it spread like wildfire. Enemy tanks were reported at Bulson, 2 miles (3 kilometres) south of Chaumont, and divisional and corps commanders below there evacuated their headquarters without even verifying the reports. Unit commanders on the front contacted their headquarters for confirmation and found them deserted, confirming their worst fears. The entire 55th Division abandoned its positions, a retreat that degenerated into a rout with the clarion call: 'The tanks are at Bulson!'

The German success has been described as the greatest tank victory in the history of warfare, which probably only slightly overstates the case. Without a doubt, the morale of the 55th had been severely mauled by the aerial bombardment, but it nevertheless held on until the reports of tanks behind their flanks came flooding in. Through the centuries troops have feared being cut off from safety – and tanks now had the potential to do this far more effectively than ever before.

Once bridgeheads had been established on the west bank of the Meuse, the panzers came into their own. Both Guderian and Rommel ordered a mad dash for the coast of the English Channel, ignoring the enemy units on their flanks. Their strategy flew in the face of all accepted sensible procedures of warfare, but it worked because the panzers' speed and their ability to brush aside all but the stiffest resistance kept the Allied defenders constantly off-balance. Major Ian English of the 7th Durham Light Infantry puts it well:

It was surprise after surprise really. Refugees hurrying to the west and then hurrying to the east because their way had been cut off in the west – rumours were rife … The tanks had the potential to catch us in a big net … The whole BEF was dancing to their tune.

His unit was ordered to relocate at least five times, on each occasion because it had been outflanked. At one point it took up a position facing towards the east near

Ypres but was forced to abandon it when shelling came in from the west. The Allied defensive system was reduced to a series of *ad hoc* decisions made by commanders in the field.

The most effective of these decisions provides a graphic demonstration of both the weakness of the blitzkrieg and the strength of the German panzer divisions. Rommel had grossly overextended himself in his desire for 7 and 8 Panzer to be the first divisions to reach the coast, and as he swept round the southern flank of Arras he was caught unawares by a hastily assembled counterattack by the British Expeditionary Force.

Lord Gort had managed to scrape together elements of the Durham Light Infantry and the 1st Army Tank Brigade plus a detachment from Prioux's 3 Division Légère Mécanique (DLM) to create a battle group known as 'Frankforce'. Under the command of Major-General Giffard le Quesne Martel, it counterattacked

After the Normandy invasion, the precarious beach-head had to be protected at all costs from German counter-attack. RAF Typhoon ground attack aircraft were particularly successful in stopping the German Panzers in their tracks. With the Luftwaffe by now effectively out of the war, the Germans were defenceless against attack from the air.

Rommel's forces on 21 May and caught his strung-out divisions in their soft underbelly throwing them into chaos. Rommel worked like a demon to restore order, bringing every available gun he had to bear on the attacking British tanks and even pressing his 88mm anti-aircraft guns into service in an anti-tank role – the first recorded instance of them being used in this way. After a shaky start, his panzer divisions pulled together and started to push back the assault.

By contrast, Frankforce suffered from bad co-ordination, inadequate radio communications and lack of combined-arms discipline. On one flank, its tanks went off in the wrong direction and left the infantry stranded; on the other, they outstripped their infantry support and were cut up piecemeal. By the evening of 21 May Rommel was able to mount a counterattack with his panzers and the Allies' Arras offensive was a spent force. Major English sums it up: 'What it amounted to was two tank battalions and two infantry battalions against two panzer divisions. It was nothing more than a pinprick, really.'

Guderian reached Boulogne on 24 May 1940, cutting off the Allied army in the Low Countries and rolling up the line. The Allies were left to salvage what they could of the BEF through Dunkirk. The German victory was one of the most spectacular ever achieved in the history of warfare and it owed much to the speed and flexibility of the panzer divisions. Never mind that most of their tanks were thin-skinned and armed with little more than popguns: once the breakthrough had been achieved, the success of the blitzkrieg lay not in head-on encounters but in sweeping, outflanking manoeuvres for which the German tanks had been specifically designed. It is a telling statistic that over half the total Allied losses in the campaign were prisoners of war who had been cut off, surrounded and forced to surrender.

THE MACHINE

AT THE HEART OF THE SUCCESS of the blitzkrieg lay the guns and caterpillar tracks of the tank. Altogether different from the lumbering monster of World War One, it was developed out of necessity to fulfil a specific role in a particular strategy – and it could only have been developed between 1919 and 1939 by the German army.

Many other armies experimented with tanks and the concept of blitzkrieg in the period between the wars. Theorists like Sir Basil Liddell Hart and Charles de Gaulle had pipe dreams of small, mobile armies made up almost entirely of armour, but by far the most influential thinker on tank theory was the chief staff officer in the fledgling British Tank Corps: Colonel John 'Boney' Fuller.

During World War One Fuller had come to realize that if tanks were more reliable and could be made to travel faster they could be used to penetrate enemy lines and destroy enemy headquarters. His theory was based on German infiltration tactics which had spread chaos through the British Fifth Army in March 1918. He set his ideas out in 'Plan 1919', a proposal to the British High Command, but the war came to an end before he had a chance to put them into practice.

The potential of this style of warfare was not lost on the German general staff. A strange body that was essentially a think tank of the most promising German officers, it acted as a form of staff college, grooming the army's élite for high command. Its ethos was one of innovative thinking grounded firmly in the traditional values of German military practice, a paradoxical mixture that was to produce some radical ideas that would change the face of war forever. Banned in 1919 by the Treaty of Versailles, it was replaced by the Truppenamt, which was the general staff in all but name. Its head was General Hans von Seeckt, a passionate advocate of mobile warfare.

Von Seeckt took the somewhat paranoid but realistic view that the next war would be fought on at least two fronts, with Germany surrounded by enemies. He therefore wanted the German army to be able to fight a delaying action on one of them while striking a hammer blow on the other. It would need to use interior lines of supply to change the point of main effort, the *Schwerpunkt*, at a moment's notice; and it would have to be able to regroup quickly and operate independently in order to react to the military situation as it developed. In this way, he hoped to hold off Germany's enemies long enough for a settlement to be negotiated on agreeable terms. Above all, he hoped to avoid the stalemate of the 1914–18 war. Inevitably, he looked towards tanks to achieve his ends.

Tanks were the bogeymen of the German army. Searching for a reason to excuse its own incompetence, the German High Command had blamed the defeat of 1918 on them. It conveniently ignored the fact that the Allies had never used tanks in significantly large concentrations, or that even their most spectacular success, at Amiens, was short-lived with most of the territory recaptured almost immediately by German infantry. It was the tank that won the war, OKH averred, and once the idea had taken hold it was difficult for German military theorists to shake it off.

These theorists were trained to think in terms of operational strategy. To put it simply, they were concerned with winning wars, not battles: get the strategy right and the battles almost looked after themselves – and the strategy drilled into the German general staff was the concept of *Vernichtens Gedanke*: 'annihilation battle'. First developed by Helmuth von Moltke in the war against Austria in 1866, it involved surrounding the enemy, severing his supply lines and then destroying him.

The advantage of the tank to this strategy is obvious. It was a mobile fighting platform. It could carry a gun and was invulnerable to small-arms fire. More important, tanks were large enough to carry the new invention of radio, which enabled them to maintain contact with other elements in the assault and co-ordinate their efforts in a manner that had not previously been possible. This gave them a huge operational advantage.

British manuals based on early tactical experiments conducted on Salisbury Plain were translated into German and distributed liberally among the officers of the Truppenamt: Colonel Charles Broad's 'Provisional Instructions for Tanks and Armoured Cars' ran to 250 copies which were eagerly devoured by tank enthusiasts in the general staff. Foremost among these was a young staff officer named Heinz Guderian.

Success is often a matter of luck and the German army was lucky that Guderian was in the right place at the right time. The nerve centre of thought on mechanized warfare was the *Inspektion der Kraftfahrtruppen* (Inspectorate of Motor Transport Troops), established by von Seeckt to co-ordinate motor transport within the German army. At its head was General Erich von Tschischwitz, a visionary who was keen to explore the potential of motorized troops and requested an officer trained in the general staff to help him.

Captain Heinz Guderian was appointed in January 1922. His experience perfectly suited him for the role. He had served as a signals officer in charge of a radio station during the early years of World War One before being promoted to staff officer at divisional and then corps level. He was therefore well-grounded in the intricacies of co-ordinating troops and had a much greater appreciation than most of the value of radio.

Initially, his work was not appreciated by his superiors. In 1924 he organized a set of exercises designed to highlight the potential of a motorized combat force but was rebuffed by von Tschischwitz's successor, Colonel von Natzmer, who said: 'To hell with combat! They are supposed to carry flour!' It was only when von Natzmer was replaced by General von Vollard-Bockelburg that serious work on tanks really started.

The Treaty of Versailles had forbidden the German army to have tanks and the theorists of armoured warfare were therefore working in a practical vacuum – Guderian, Germany's foremost thinker on the subject, would not set foot inside a tank until he visited Sweden in 1929. In 1926 Vollard-Bockelburg set out to rectify the situation. He converted the inspectorate into the *Kraftfahrkampftruppen* (Motorized Combat Troops), and concluded an agreement with the Soviet Union that enabled Germany and the USSR to hold joint tank trials near the Russian town of Kazan.

However, trials could not take place until the German army had tanks, and in 1926 plans for the first experimental vehicles since World War One were drawn up. They were built in secret in Russia and called 'tractors' to fool the Allies. There were two designs. The *Grosstraktor* (heavy tractor) held a crew of six and a 75mm

gun. It weighed about 20 tons and was designed to have a maximum speed of 30 miles (48 kilometres) an hour. Three firms – Krupp, Rheinmetall-Borsig and Daimler-Benz – were contracted to build two *Grosstraktoren* each but the job was so technically difficult in the prevailing atmosphere of secrecy and economic hardship that it was two years before the first *Grosstraktor* rolled off the production line. The design for a *Leichter Traktor* (light tractor) weighing about 12 tons was also approved in 1926, but its development took even longer.

Many strategists in the German army of the 1930s were looking at radical ways to fight a multi-front war, and Guderian was not the only one who saw tanks as the way forward or understood the potential of all-arms formations. Indeed, the synergy of combined arms was a concept that had become ingrained in the general staff. It was a goal in itself: the holy grail of German operational strategy. Yet in many ways, Guderian was the brightest and most successful of all of them: he was right about tanks, he was right about combined arms, and he was right about the importance of radio. However, his ideas were tempered by the wise counsel of

Victory at last. Street by street, building by building, cellar by cellar, the Soviets pummelled their way to the heart of Hitler's Berlin. With the Red Flag now flying from the roof of the Reichstag, it was all over. A few hundred yards away lay Hitler's petrol-soaked corpse. It had cost 15 million Russian lives, but the war was now over.

others like Major-General Oswald Lutz and von Tschischwitz and limited by German capabilities. It seems likely that Guderian would otherwise have made the classic mistake of including too many tanks in the panzer divisions.

By 1933, the ingredients were in place for a major revolution in military practice. All that was required was the catalyst. And that catalyst was Adolf Hitler. Riding the crest of a wave of public nationalism fomented by Nazi propaganda, he ordered the rearmament of Germany. The army needed no further prompting.

Conceived as an interim training vehicle, the first tank to be built in Germany was originally labelled the *Landwirtschaftlicher Schlepper* (LaS) or 'agricultural tractor'; but it was an agricultural tractor with two machine-guns in a hand-cranked turret and enough armour to defend against small-arms fire. Designed by Krupp, its electro-welded hull weighed about 5 tons and carried a two-man crew. The early model IA had suspension problems and its original Krupp engine proved inadequate. The contract was transferred to Daimler-Benz, who gave it a more powerful engine and a leaf-suspension system that enabled it to reach a top speed of 30 miles (48 kilometres) an hour on good roads. By that time all attempt at pretence had been dropped and it was given the name familiar to all *aficionados* of armoured warfare: the armoured fighting vehicle or *Panzerkampfwagen I*.

The first Panzer I rolled off the production line in 1934 and was put through its paces at the tank-proving grounds in Kummersdorf. Hitler came to see one in action and was greatly impressed. As it manoeuvred over and around the obstacles set for it, he pointed at the little machine and exclaimed: 'That's what I need! That's what I want to have!' The future of the panzer was assured. Over two thousand Panzer Is were built, 96 of which took part in the invasion of France.

The panzer strategy developed by Lutz and Guderian called for a main battle-tank armed with an armour-piercing gun capable of knocking out enemy armour, backed up on a ratio of three to one by a medium-support tank with a lower-velocity gun capable of firing high-explosive rounds to suppress enemy infantry. In May 1940 these roles were nominally filled by the PzKpfw III and the PzKpfw IV.

The Daimler-Benz design for the PzKpfw III incorporated several features that were at the cutting edge of tank technology. It had an improved layout for an all-seated five-man crew (the commander and gunner in earlier tanks had to stand), a 10-speed pre-selector gearbox (which proved to be overly complicated and was eventually replaced), 90mm of frontal armour and a 350 horsepower engine capable of a road-speed of up to 25 miles (40 kilometres) an hour. Its turret mounted a 37mm PAK anti-tank gun that was identical to the one used by infantry anti-tank units so that ammunition could be swapped between them as and when required, and the turret ring was made deliberately large to allow for an upgrading of the gun as weapons technology improved – a feature that was to give the PzKpfw III at least two more years serviceable life than it would otherwise have enjoyed. Most important, it was fitted with Dr Ferdinand Porsche's revolutionary new torsion-bar suspension system, which was to become standard on most German tanks after 1940.

Suspension governs a tank's performance over uneven terrain and affects its road-speed. Good suspension enables it to surmount much more difficult obstacles than a similar vehicle with an inferior system. It also cuts down on the wear and tear of vital running parts and adds to the tank's theoretical range. One of the main disadvantages of the World War One tanks was that they were jerky, jolting machines that were likely to get stuck on uneven ground and eventually juddered themselves apart. The beauty of Porsche's torsion bar was that it not only improved performance, but also that it was protected by the tank wheels, rendering it much less vulnerable to anti-tank fire.

Torsion-bar suspension was what allowed the distinctive, overlapping wheel system of later German tanks.

The PzKpfw IV was the natural progression from the PzKpfw II and did not at first use the torsion bar. Ordered in 1935, it entered production in 1937 – one year earlier than its technical predecessor, the PzKpfw III. Like the PzKpfw III, it held a crew of five, three of whom operated in a spacious turret that was, for the first time, electronically powered. Its short 75mm gun fired a high-explosive round but could also load an armour-piercing projectile. It was capable of over 30 miles (48 kilometres) an hour on the road – speedy for a medium tank – and was reliable and versatile, with a turret large enough to be up-gunned, enough armour to give the vehicle adequate protection against enemy firepower, and the capacity for more to be fitted as required. These features gave the PzKpfw IV the distinction of being the only German tank to see service throughout the whole war.

Mechanically, panzers were markedly superior to their Allied counterparts. All had an electro-welded body-shell that was stronger than one held together with rivets which often snapped loose under fire and added to bullet splash inside the tank. Their tracks were specifically developed for long-distance road travel, and the torsion-bar suspension gave a great leap forward in performance. Even the leaf springs of the PzKpfw I, II and IV had the advantage of simplicity. In contrast, the suspension of the Matilda MkII, the best British tank, was a nightmare of levers and springs. As David Fletcher of Bovington Tank Museum has said: 'It was good for a watch – not for a tank.' The panzers' optical sights were also much better than those in Allied tanks and this, combined with the German practice of firing while stationary, made the vehicles much more accurate and deadly than those of their opponents.

Furthermore, while the standard German battle tank had a five-man crew seated in a spacious turret that gave the commander a good field of view and allowed him to watch the battle develop, the corresponding Allied one usually contained only three men and the commander, who had to stand, and was also the gunner. In addition, every German panzer contained a radio, although only the command tank could transmit as well as receive. Allied radio was usually limited to the battalion commander and German command and control was therefore far superior to that of the Allies.

Command and control could be exerted on an all-arms force of tanks, infantry, engineers, artillery, anti-tank guns and, most important of all, aircraft to bring down concentrated fire on any area identified by the divisional commander. And once a breakthrough had been achieved the panzer came into its own, pushing speedily into the Allies' rear echelons, avoiding head-on confrontations wherever possible and encircling the enemy who could then be rolled up at leisure with the help of the more prosaic infantry divisions that followed the tanks.

Lutz and Guderian had laid down the basic structure of the panzer division by 1934 and in 1935 it faced its first big test in exercises on Luenberg Heath. General Werner von Fritsch, the commander-in-chief of the exercise, ordered it to make a 90-degree turn to face an enemy who had appeared on its flank. It was an inordinately complicated manoeuvre, under incredible pressure, but within 85 minutes the prototype panzer division had turned to face the attack and was mounting its own counterthrust. Luenberg Heath had once and for all proven the value of combined arms to a sceptical world. By 1938 Lutz's command contained three fledgeling panzer divisions and had become the XVI Army Korps.

Guderian and Lutz now had a force that was capable of mounting a lightning strike against any predetermined point and that could exploit the breakthrough in a rapid and flexible encircling manoeuvre that would have made von Moltke proud. With the annexation of Czechoslovakia in March 1939, they gained another 1000-plus tanks and the invasion of Poland ironed the last wrinkles out of the strategy. The scene was now set for their biggest test and the ultimate prize. The prize was France, and the test was the total destruction of the French army.

THE VERDICT

ON 8 JULY 1941, 17 days into Operation Barbarossa, the German invasion of the Soviet Union, the men of 17 Panzer Division near the River Dnepr noticed a single, unfamiliar Russian tank emerging from a cornfield. They opened fire but were horrified to see their shells ricochet off as it began to advance. It tore a swath 9 miles (14.5 kilometres) deep through the German lines before it was stopped by a 100mm artillery shell fired from behind. A similar story was being enacted up and down the front. Guderian, now commander of the German forces in Russia, went to photograph a pair of the tanks whose advance had been halted only when they

THE PANZER AND THE T-34

The Germans resorted to building huge, complicated new tanks to counter the simple, and effective T-34. Although capable of destroying a T-34 in one-to-one combat, they were cumbersome, slow, and too few in number. T-34s would simply charge the Germans at point blank range. Casualties were very high on both sides. Slowly and surely the Red Army broke through

The Germans saw this as an almost religious war. The Nazis hated the Bolsheviks and wanted to reduce the whole of the Soviet Union to ashes, enslaving the population and routing all opposition. They ruthlessly murdered millions of civilians, prisoners and Jews, even those Russians who were opposed to Stalin. The war on the Russian Front was the bloodiest of the whole war, by far – 20 million Russians and 7 million Germans died.

The T-34 took the Germans completely by surprise. It had been developed in total secrecy, and built in vast new factories in the east, which the Russians had moved out of the path of the advancing Germans. Faster, more powerful, robust, and with an engine able to operate in sub-zero temperatures, it led the Russian assault on the Germans. In 1945, it was the T-34 tank that led the Red Army all the way to Berlin.

For every German tank replacing one destroyed, the Soviets would get five

German mobile anti-tank gun

76mm cannon

Shell cases

Sloping front armour – shells would bounce off harmlessly

Forward machine-gun

3-man crew

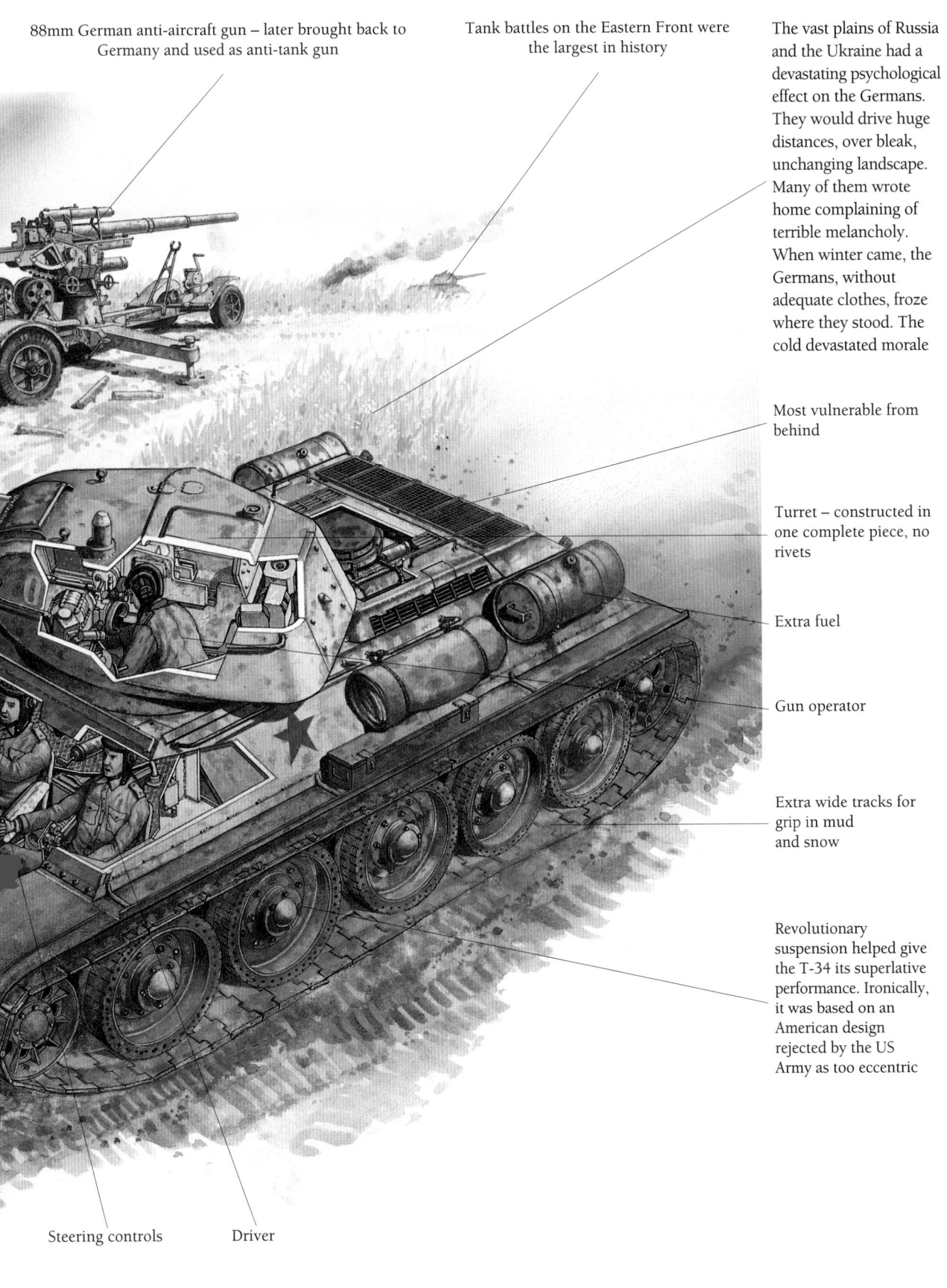

88mm German anti-aircraft gun – later brought back to Germany and used as anti-tank gun

Tank battles on the Eastern Front were the largest in history

The vast plains of Russia and the Ukraine had a devastating psychological effect on the Germans. They would drive huge distances, over bleak, unchanging landscape. Many of them wrote home complaining of terrible melancholy. When winter came, the Germans, without adequate clothes, froze where they stood. The cold devastated morale

Most vulnerable from behind

Turret – constructed in one complete piece, no rivets

Extra fuel

Gun operator

Extra wide tracks for grip in mud and snow

Revolutionary suspension helped give the T-34 its superlative performance. Ironically, it was based on an American design rejected by the US Army as too eccentric

Steering controls

Driver

had accidentally driven into a marsh. It was the first time he had ever seen a T-34.

It is one of World War Two's great ironies that the Germans failed to learn from their victory of 1940. The attack on France had been so swift and so successful that the inherent weakness of blitzkrieg was largely ignored. The strategy worked best – it is arguable that it only worked at all – if the psychological impact of tanks could be combined with surprise and a lighting attack on a defined objective, cutting off an enemy force and intimidating it into surrender. On the Russian Front objectives were thousands of miles apart and the Russian soldier simply refused to admit defeat. The German army won Pyrrhic victory after Pyrrhic victory, but the 'tank terror' was all on its side, as its soldiers came to realize that the standard PAK 37mm gun used in the Panzer IIIs and their anti-tank units could not penetrate the T-34's armour. Meanwhile, the Russian High Command was learning from the German mistakes and refining its strategy slowly but inexorably – moulding it around its tank.

The T-34 was a wonder of basic engineering. Designed by Mikhail Koshkin, the wunderkind of the Leningrad OKMO tank design bureau, it amalgamated all the best elements of British, American and German tank design of the 1930s with lessons learned from the Spanish Civil War and Russia's inter-war conflict with Japan. Koshkin and his team concentrated on the bare essentials: guns, armour and

German tanks saw action in all theatres of war. A PzKpfw III surrenders to some British 'Desert Rats' in North Africa. Note the distinctive 'Afrika Korps' equipment racks on the rear of the tank.

mobility, jettisoning anything that might slow the tank's production or impair its operational efficiency. The original cumbersome Christie wheel-and-track suspension was jettisoned in favour of the torsion bar; the front armour was sloped in order to deflect armour-piercing shells; the turret was cast in one piece rather than being welded out of cold-rolled steel; and a diesel engine that reduced the risk of explosion and was remarkably resistant to the Siberian cold was installed.

Like the Allied tanks, the T-34 had several design flaws, most notably a cramped turret that required the commander to act as the gunner and a marked lack of radio communication. But its simplicity proved its greatest advantage. It was reliable in all Russian weathers, easy to mass-produce and had a top speed of 35 miles (56 kilometres) an hour with a range of almost 300 miles (480 kilometres). Its crews possessed a macho disdain for the more luxurious but temperamental PzKpfw IIIs that were issued to some Soviet tank units.

The original design concept called for 45mm of frontal armour and an L-11 76.2mm gun. This was eventually upgraded to 60mm and a Grabin F-34 76.2mm. Along with its low profile and sloping armour, this made the Russian tank tougher and more deadly than its closest German counterpart. It was designated the T-34/76 after the year its design was commissioned and the calibre of the gun it carried. Its designer never lived to see it in action: he died of pneumonia on 26 September 1940.

National pride meant that the Germans could not countenance copying the design of the T-34 – their initial panic reaction to its advent on the Russian front. Besides, the aluminium engine used by Koshkin could not be mass-produced in Germany. Instead, they came up with an alternative, the PzKpfw 'Panther', which improved on many of the Russian tank's design features. It took two years to produce the Panther and in the interim the army up-gunned its Panzer IIIs and IVs and introduced the PAK 40 75mm anti-tank gun.

Although the Panther was in production by March 1943 it had not undergone extensive field tests. Nevertheless, Hitler decreed that it, along with the new Tiger I, should be committed against the Russian salient at the industrial city of Kursk. Heinz Guderian, now inspector-general of armoured forces, argued against this maintaining that the army should spend a year consolidating its panzer divisions, but was overruled. 'Operation Citadel' would go ahead in July and would prove to be the largest armoured offensive ever mounted in history. There is a certain poetic symmetry in the knowledge that the man placed in overall command of this, the death knell of the German blitzkrieg, was its architect of 1940: Field Marshal Fritz von Manstein.

In essence, the task at Kursk was simple. The city lay at the centre of a giant bulge, 70 miles (112 kilometres) wide, in the Soviet line created by the Russians' winter campaign of 1942. Hitler called for a pincer movement targeted on Kursk from north and south, and committed 36 divisions including 13 panzer divisions

Soviet soldiers inspect the wreckage of a German tank in the aftermath of Kursk, the largest tank battle in history. Although superior to the T-34, later German tanks were too heavy, too unreliable and too dependent on spare parts to be able to stop the Soviet advance.

with 2700 tanks and assault guns to the effort. Against them was ranged a Soviet army that had learned how to deal with the blitzkrieg and had painstakingly constructed a combined-arms strategy of its own. This hinged on the 1930s Russian strategy of 'deep operations', the objective of which was to disrupt and destroy enemy cohesion through a series of smashing hammer blows. Over 40 000 mines had been laid to channel the German offensive into a series of '*pakfronts*' that stretched to a depth of over 12 miles (19 kilometres) and contained more than 6000 anti-tank guns hidden in ambush.

Even before the panzers advanced into this field of death, their assault was disrupted by a massive Soviet bombardment of their assembly areas. Like lambs to the slaughter, they drove into the trap set for them and were butchered wholesale. Panthers that were not destroyed proved unreliable and broke down in an ignominious baptism of fire. The northern offensive ground to a halt before it had progressed 10 miles (16 kilometres), and took six days to cover even that distance. To the south, von Manstein fared somewhat better and punched a 'fist' of 700 tanks, including the SS Panzer grenadier units Liebstandarte Adolf Hitler, Das Reich and Totenkopf, through the Soviet lines on 5 July. By 12 July they had fought their way some 20 miles (32 kilometres) into the Kursk salient and were threatening a breakthrough when the Soviet Union's Marshal Nikolay Vatutin ordered the 5th Guards Tank Army under Lieutenant-General Rotmistrov to counterattack at the village of Prokhorovka.

It was the largest tank battle ever fought and probably the most desperate. Unable to penetrate the frontal armour of either the Tiger or the Panther, the Russian T-34s simply charged at top speed into the advancing panzer formations and sought to engage them at point-blank range. On the German left flank, 3 SS Totenkopf was assailed on two sides and almost annihilated. Across the battlefield the death toll in mangled machines on both sides rose to 700. The Soviets lost over 50 per cent of their armoured force, but they broke the back of the panzer divisions and were able to replace their machines at a much faster rate than the Germans.

The Russians went immediately on to the offensive, and the difference in style between their attacks in the north and the south is illuminating. To the north of Kursk, they launched what was essentially an unsuccessful blitzkrieg on the Orel bulge. The intention had been to break through the German line and encircle its forces, but the assault degenerated into a painful slog and it took the Soviets three weeks to push the Germans back some 75 miles (120 kilometres). By the time they had regrouped for an offensive to the south of the city, they had learned their lesson and refined their strategy. 'Operation Rumantsyev' on the 3 August was a series of sequential attacks across a front of over 18 miles (30 kilometres) which sent the Germans reeling back to Kharkov and Gadyach over 100 miles (160 kilometres) away and which formed the basis for nearly all subsequent Soviet armoured offensives. The German army had begun a retreat that would only end in Berlin.

The battle of Kursk ended for ever the myth of the German panzer and exposed the weaknesses of the blitzkrieg. But the tank was not obsolete and combined-arms operations were not dead. Russian-made T-34s would participate in an Israeli blitzkrieg during the Six Day War of 1967, and General Norman Schwarzkopf would use a combination of blitzkrieg encirclement and deep operations strategy in the final United States offensive against the forces of Saddam Hussein in the Gulf.

Using tanks like this, the Germans overran continental Europe in under a year.
Combined with dive-bombers and storm-troopers, there was BLITZKRIEG,
literally, lightning war.

Yet it is perhaps fitting that the final words on the blitzkrieg should be those of General Hoth to General Fritz von Manstein, the architect of the strategy, in the aftermath of Kursk: 'The Russians have learned a lot since 1941. They are no longer peasants with simple minds. They have learned the art of war from us.'

Columns like this, miles in length, had crossed the Soviet Border in the Summer of 1941, Operation Barbarossa. Three years later, they were going the other way, back to Germany, in one of the most protracted and bloody retreats in World War Two. Four-fifths of the German Army fought on the Eastern Front, and millions died.

CHAPTER 4

THE P-51 MUSTANG

That's the plane I want!

GENERAL CARL SPAATZ,
COMMANDING OFFICER OF THE
8TH AIR FORCE, SEEING THE
MUSTANG PRODUCTION LINE

The first time your bombers came over
Hanover escorted by fighters, I began to
be worried. When they came with
fighter escort over Berlin – I knew
the jig was up.

FIELD MARSHAL HERMANN GOERING,
GERMAN COMMISSIONER FOR AVIATION

THE CHALLENGE

BY SPRING 1944 World War Two was five years old. The Allies were still in the planning stages for D-Day, the great – and highly risky – invasion of continental Europe. The Red Army was beginning its push into the Ukraine against desperate German resistance. The tide was turning, but still the end seemed as far away as ever. Germany was waging total war, its resolve to defend home territory undiminished. Armament production was still rising, even though the factories that manufactured the weapons were pounded by bombs, day and night. The civilian population was battered but unbroken. And Hitler was still secure in absolute power despite the attempt to assassinate him on 20 July. Fortress Europe was unbreached.

In the end, defeat would come from the two great weapons of the war: tanks from the East, and heavy bombers from the West. Behind both of them was the poor bloody infantry, who finally win all wars, slogging their way, bridge by bridge, street by street, to the heart of the Nazi Reich. Both the Allies – and the more prescient Germans – knew as early as 1943 that the Nazis had squandered any real chance of victory, but that defeat would nevertheless be inflicted only by taking the battle to Germany. And air power was the only way the Allies could do it.

Allied bombers had been flying over German-held territory in large numbers since 1942, testament to the enduring faith that the British and Americans, alone of all the participants in World War Two, placed in the power of the long-range, four-engined bomber. The Germans had flirted with the idea, but had insisted that any prototype should also be able to dive-bomb. The three years of fruitless development this had entailed meant no equivalent of the Lancaster or Flying Fortress was ever built by the Axis powers. Neither Japan nor, on the Allied side, the Soviet Union saw any use in this type of aircraft, and concentrated on producing fighters and aircraft-carrier-borne dive-bombers respectively. It was left to the United States Air Force (USAF) to theorize about the use of bombers, and the Royal Air Force (RAF) to pioneer the tactics of deploying them.

Hopes that these huge lumbering giants would be able to deliver a knock-out Armageddon blow to the enemy were cruelly dashed in the first days of the war. RAF Stirlings and Wellingtons, slow and able to operate only at medium altitude,

A Mustang escorting a formation of B-17 Flying Fortresses. Bomber crews wanted the comfort of the fighters flying close at hand. Mustang pilots disagreed. Instead they would fly at a distance, ready to pounce on attacking German interceptors.

were being knocked out of the sky. The RAF was forced to abandon flying in daylight and to fly only at night, which meant that the bombers' already limited accuracy was diminished still further. Intelligence research showed that hardly one bomb in ten was landing within miles of its intended target. But the British persevered; they had no other way of striking back at the triumphant Germans.

In 1942 the Americans set up their 8th Air Force under General Carl Spaatz with the express intention of conducting a campaign of intense and deadly daylight bombing of key German targets. Spaatz's confidence in both the technology and the tactics was undaunted despite the British experience. At the Casablanca Conference in January 1943 the Americans and British had resolved to lay the ground for D-Day and for Operation Torch (the invasion of Europe from the south through Italy) with: '... the progressive destruction and dislocation of the German military, industrial and economic system, and the undermining of the morale of the German people to a point where their capacity for armed resistance is fatally weakened.'

After the conference, President Franklin D. Roosevelt (despite having earlier been an outspoken critic of bombing) and the British prime minister, Winston Churchill, committed the Allies to a sustained campaign of land bombing as the necessary prelude to the invasion of Europe, which Joseph Stalin, the Soviet Communist leader, had forced them to promise for 1944.

Both the British and the Americans had at least laid the ground for this strategy. Boeing, the American aircraft giant, had developed the B-17 Flying Fortress in the mid-1930s as the United States' front-line bomber. Designed to fly at high altitude – it had a ceiling of 35 000 feet (10 600 metres), 10 000 feet (3000 metres) higher than the RAF Lancaster – and delivered a payload of 10 000 pounds (4500 kilograms) of bombs, it had a range easily capable of reaching Berlin. Its name was not fanciful either. This was a bomber designed to be impossible to shoot down. Bristling with fully automated swivelling turrets, each armed with 50-calibre machine-guns, and firing in every direction, the B-17s flew in tight formations: the bomber group was an aerial porcupine that would curl into a ball with sharpened quills deterring all but the most reckless enemy fighter. Or that was the theory.

The sad truth was that the RAF had not chosen to fly at night from whim. By the end of 1942 German air defences were highly developed, and very effective. The Americans would have to endure the same learning curve as their British counterparts, the same early blooding in the realities of mass formation twentieth-century aerial warfare. The air war was in reality a terrible undertaking. To get to Germany the bombers had to cross the formidable 'Kammhuber line', a defensive system of co-ordinated radar, fighter squadrons and flak (50 000 radar-directed anti-aircraft guns). The Luftwaffe had developed and refined its anti-bomber strategy, stationing up to 70 per cent of all its fighters in the Western theatre.

Scrambled as soon as the radar picked up the huge formations flying east, squadrons of Me 109s, FW 190s, twin-engined Me 110s and Junkers Ju-88 'destroyers', carrying both cannon and airborne rockets, would stalk the bombers and attack them at high speed, often head-on. The formation 'boxes' of tightly packed B-17s, huddled together for protection, would quickly disintegrate. Bombers that were damaged or fell behind would be picked off by rocket and cannon. For all its gun turrets and machine-guns, the B-17 proved as slow and vulnerable as its British counterpart, and like the British before them, the Americans were being shot to ribbons on ill-fated missions.

Fortunately for the Allies, the hubristic Hitler was ill-disposed to think defensively and ranked air defence a low priority. His reluctance to commit greater resources to this was vital in allowing the Allied air forces the chance to establish a foothold in the skies above Germany, and provided them with the incentive to persevere with the strategy that was costing so many lives. Nevertheless, it was clear that even as late as 1943 the upper hand was with the Luftwaffe who were, after all, fighting to save their homeland. This was their Battle of Britain and like the Spitfires and Hurricanes of the RAF's Fighter Command, the Messerschmitts and Focke-Wulfs fought a desperate and merciless battle.

The extent of the Luftwaffe edge became very clear to the 8th Air Force when it mounted its first deep-penetration raids in the spring and summer of 1943. For all their swagger and bellicose faith in the power of daylight precision bombing, the Americans were losing up to 30 planes, each with a crew of ten, on an average raid.

On the first anniversary of the 8th Air Force's arrival in England, American bombers flew even deeper into Germany, bombing the Focke-Wulf plant south of Berlin and the ball-bearing plants at Schweinfurt. Sixty planes failed to return. All the way from Antwerp to their targets and back again, the hapless bombers were 'bounced' by German fighters who used every trick they knew, attacking from every direction, diving out of the sun, charging them head on, from underneath, from behind – whatever it took. Two weeks later it happened again. The Luftwaffe were now masters of their deadly defensive tactics. A further 60 out of 300 Flying Fortresses were destroyed and 138 badly damaged. The Americans had no choice but to suspend operations even though the bombers had managed to inflict enormous damage. Albert Speer, the German armaments minister, later conceded that just one more raid on the Schweinfurt plant would have crippled him. As it was, ball-bearings, vital for tank production, once again poured off German production lines. It was a classic wartime dilemma; the strategy was sound, but it was costing too many lives.

The objective of the bombing was to defeat the German nation – not just its military forces – in two ways. Carpet bombing at night, now being carried out with greater effectiveness by the Lancasters of the RAF, which were equipped with new target-identifying radar systems and able to fly in co-ordinated formations, was designed to bring the war to the homeland and crush civilian morale. American

precision bombing by day was intended to cripple the enemy's industrial infrastructure.

Allied strategy did not include taking on Germany's military forces directly. The Luftwaffe was not the primary target – yet it was the Luftwaffe that was winning the battle. By the winter of 1943–44 the Allies were compelled to rethink the campaign. The conclusion was inevitable: until the German fighters were destroyed, the bombers would fail in their missions and the Allies would never realistically have a chance of invading Europe by 1944. The war would remain at stalemate. There would be no D-Day, and Stalin would be the principal architect of German defeat, the Americans and the British his useless junior partners. The Americans had foreseen this as early as 1941, but the British had been sceptical. In fact the disagreement was academic. Only the Americans had the wherewithal to make daylight bombing work and take the war to the Germans, so it was just as well that they recognized the need to do it. General Henry 'Hap' Arnold, commander of the American Air Force (AAF), sent this message to his

An early model of the Mustang, with its distinctive 'greenhouse' canopy, and all-over olive drab camouflage. It was first used as a medium altitude reconnaissance and ground attack aircraft. Only later did the Allies discover that its range and performance would make it the war's most effective bomber escort.

commanders: 'My personal message to you – this is a MUST – is to "Destroy the Enemy Air Force wherever you find them in the air, on the ground, and in the factories".'

The Americans faced two overwhelming military priorities. First, to provide protection for their bombers deep over Germany, ideally all the way to Berlin which was now the Allies' most important target; and second, to destroy the Luftwaffe 'on the ground and in the factories'. As luck would have it, one fighter enabled them to do both. It was the legendary P-51 Mustang.

THE BATTLE

THE P-51 WAS THE MOST powerful and versatile piston-engined fighter of the war. It excelled as a dive-bomber, ground attack aircraft and reconnaissance plane. It saw service in many of the world's air forces for years after the war. But it made military history in one particular capacity: as 'little friend', or long-range bomber escort. And the key to the Mustang's success was a simple development: the external, pressurized drop tank. All American fighters used these tanks routinely in transit flights from the United States to Britain. But they compromised performance and were therefore thought to be unsuitable for combat. The Americans thought again; why not use the tanks?

Indeed, why not? Mustangs carrying the 108 gallon (490 litre) drop tanks could fly well into German airspace before having to jettison them and revert to their large internal tanks for combat and the return journey. Thus equipped, the P-51 became the only single-engined fighter capable of flying the 1200 mile (1930 kilometre) round trip from the bases in East Anglia and Cambridgeshire to Berlin and back.(The Japanese 'Zero' could fly further, but only without armour and very slowly.)

But just being able to fly a long way was in itself useless. The planes also had to win dogfights above Germany's burning cities, against the best fighter aces in the Luftwaffe when they got there – and still have enough fuel to get home. Again the Mustang triumphed. As well as stamina, it had speed and manoeuvrability. Once freed of its drop tanks, it flew 50 miles (80 kilometres) an hour faster than the FW 190, the Luftwaffe's best fighter and scourge of the bombers. It could outclimb and outdive the Me 109. Only the Me 262, Germany's twin-engined jet interceptor, could fly faster, but thanks to the tardiness of its production, and Hitler's by now usual inability to accept the advice of his technicians (he insisted they develop it as a bomber and not as a fighter), its impact was marginal.

But it was the Mustang's stamina that really astonished the Allies – and the German pilots who had become accustomed to shooting down sitting-duck bombers unmolested. It could stay in the air for up to 8 hours, four times longer than the British Spitfire, with whom it shared the Merlin engine. It was not the first plane the Americans had developed as a bomber escort, but it was the best.

The Mustang's predecessors and rivals were the great gas-guzzling P-47 Thunderbolt, and the sleek, twin-hulled P-38 Lightning. Both had patrolled the skies of northern Europe protecting the bombers. Their impact had been considerable. Goering had not believed the reports telling him that P-47s had been spotted above Aachen; 'a freak wind' was responsible, he insisted, sticking his head back in the sand. P-38s and P-47s took the bombers as far as they were able – not much further than across the German frontier – then turned back, low on fuel, abandoning the 'big friends' to their lonely fate. Neither aircraft was therefore ideal. The Thunderbolt, or 'Jug', was unwieldy and, even with external fuel tanks, too thirsty to have sufficient range. The P-38 suffered at altitude and was chronically unreliable. When it became obvious by 1944 that the B-17 Flying Fortresses, now joined by the new but less glamorous B-24 Liberators, would have to fly to Berlin and beyond, the 8th Air Force needed a better plane to escort them and it was to the Mustang that they turned. As one group commander, Colonel Hubert Zemke put it:

> P-51. By far the best air-to-air fighter aircraft of the three [the P-51, P-47 and P-38] below 25 000 feet. It had a very good radius of action for the type of work we did in Europe. The acceleration from slow cruise to maximum performance was excellent compared with that of the competition. Its rate of roll was good and it manoeuvred easily to a learned hand. Dive and acceleration were rapid, visibility in all directions was ample. As an instrument-flying aircraft it was a bit touchy, and it could easily be over-controlled in turbulence. On the question of armament, it carried sufficient machine-guns. Why I say this is that after viewing numerous combat films where pilots fired at extreme range or over-deflected, I came firmly to a conclusion that one should fight for a combat position of 10 degrees or less deflection. At close range – 250 yards or less – there is no doubt what would happen when the trigger was depressed: it was a matter of ducking the flying pieces after that.

It fell to Zemke's rival, Lieutenant-Colonel Don Blakeslee, to find out whether he was right: he became the first American fighter commander to take the Mustang to the 'big B' – Berlin. Could the bombers get through with long-range escort?

On 4 March 1944 Lieutenant-Colonel Blakeslee strapped himself into the cockpit of his P-51D Mustang. His was the first of 48 red-nosed aircraft lining up for take-off early that morning. One by one, their engines caught and they moved into position

on the runway. So far, so routine, only this time they were going to fly further into Germany than any single-engined plane had ever done – all the way to Berlin.

After taking off they set course across the English Channel, and headed for their rendezvous point with the 8th Air Force B-17 bombers, taking over escort duties from the P-47 Thunderbolts which were already low on fuel. It was a murky, gloomy day, and the weather was deteriorating. The Mustangs were forced to climb high above the solid black cloud. Problems with their oxygen supplies forced some to turn back. The remainder soon picked up their bombers, and took up positions above and in front of them. It was only as the B-17s dropped their bombs over the Reich capital that they met the first wave of German fighters.

Blakeslee and his flight were soon in the thick of savage dogfights over Berlin, diving into a group of Focke-Wulfs and Messerschmitts. With a German plane in his sights, Blakeslee opened up – and nothing happened. His guns had iced up during the long high-altitude flight. It was reported that he and the German had waved to each other; Blakeslee later contemptuously said 'if he had waved I would have rammed him'. As it was, the German was only too happy to dive for cover, and Blakeslee would have to wait for his first victim over Berlin. Lieutenant Charles Anderson dodged and weaved his way through clouds full of FW 190s. Captain Nicholas 'Cowboy' Megura pursued one right down to ground level, flying straight and low over Berlin's roof-tops. After destroying a plane on the tarmac of an airfield, he set off for home. The Mustangs did not lose a single plane.

In Goering's words, 'The jig was up.' The Americans knew this, and wanted to press home their advantage. Two days later they launched a 15 mile (24 kilometre) wave of bombers aimed at Berlin. Four hours later it turned into one of the war's greatest air battles, with over two thousand aircraft above Hitler's capital. This time it was the Americans who learnt a bitter lesson. Just having an escort of Mustangs was not enough; the planes had to be in the right place. Unfortunately, on 6 March there was a fatal gap between the lead squadron of Mustangs and the rear one. German radar operators spotted it and funnelled their fighters through the middle. The result was the rout of one entire bomber group, with 20 planes shot down in under half an hour. By the end of the day, 69 bombers had failed to return. The lesson was clear: any chink in the protective Mustang shield would be fatal. The P-51s never made that mistake again.

The next time Colonel Blakeslee's fighters flew above Berlin there was more for them to cheer about. His Mustangs were part of a force of over eight hundred fighters alongside P-47s and P-38s and 81 enemy aircraft were destroyed for 11

PREVIOUS SPREAD: *The final version of the Mustang, with its teardrop shaped Plexiglas canopy. This one has its D-Day striped markings. By this stage in the war, with complete mastery of the skies, the Mustang could dispense with camouflage, and retain the buffed silver it left the factory with.*

American losses. After a shaky start to the Mustang's career as a long-range fighter over Berlin, this was to become the dominant pattern.

Squadrons of Mustangs, Jugs and (decreasingly) Lightnings would take off from their bases and take up their positions near the bombers lumbering east. Flying first on fuselage tanks to preserve their centre of gravity, the Mustangs would switch to their drop tanks for the 2½ hour flight to Berlin, zig-zagging high above the bombers. Like the Luftwaffe before them, the 8th Air Force had discovered that fighters were most effectively deployed away from bombers, ready to dive and pounce on interceptors. Bomber crews hated having to forfeit the comfort of Mustangs flying alongside them, and there was considerable disagreement between senior air force personnel before the strategy was authorized.

American confidence grew during March and April 1944. Raids striking deep into Germany were mounted every few days. The Luftwaffe, though reeling, was far from being a spent force and showed every sign of fighting to the end. On 16 March the Americans attacked Augsburg and Friedrichshafen and 75 German fighters were shot down by P-51s. Individual Mustang groups were soon claiming victories in triple figures, unheard of earlier in the war, achieved at a ratio of six to one in their favour, and boasted many new 'aces' – anyone credited with five confirmed kills or more. In a decisive air battle on 18 April 128 German planes were destroyed, in the air as well as on the ground. 'Hap' Arnold's words were coming true. The Luftwaffe was being mauled over northern Europe, and bombers were increasingly dictating the course of the war. D-Day was back on the agenda. Now it was only a matter of choosing a date, and the Allies would be in Europe.

Escort duties evolved specific strategies. Unlike the German interceptors, Mustang pilots sat in cramped cockpits for up to 7 or 8 hours, flying at extremely high altitudes, and fighting both the cold (-50 degrees Centigrade at 35 000 feet/ 10 600 metres) that played havoc with their in-flight systems, and the exhaustion caused by breathing pressurized oxygen.

When action did finally happen, it did so explosively. A pilot's sky would suddenly be full of planes, German and American. The FWs would strafe the B-17s, weaving their way through the cordons of defensive fire and opening the way for the slower rocket-carrying Me 110s who would follow in for the kill. They would rake the bombers with bursts of machine-gun fire, and oil, coolant and shards of aluminium and Plexiglas would be punched out of airframes and into the sky. The beleaguered Fortresses would sway and buckle, leaking smoke and hydraulics, breaking up before cartwheeling out of control. If they were lucky the 10-man crew would have seconds to bale out. If not, they burned up with their planes. Trails of debris would bring every other German fighter in the vicinity to finish off the damaged bomber.

It would now be the Mustangs' turn to join battle. The pilot's gun sight would fill – for seconds only – as German fighters dived, spun and swung away.

Calculating range and deflection, the Mustang pilot's six 50-calibre machine-guns would pepper the sky, seeking out the fuselage, fuel tanks, ailerons and cockpit of his enemy. The sky would be full of targets and keeping any of them in his sights long enough to shoot was a problem. Air combat was short and deadly. As one pilot put it: 'Two seconds later, one of you would be dead.' The German fighters were armed with bomber-busting 30mm cannon, one shell of which would incinerate a single-engined fighter, so the Mustang too was vulnerable to attack.

Craning round to scour the sky, the Mustang pilot had continually to check behind and above him. He was only seconds away from being torn apart by enemy gunfire. Nudging his stick left and right, diving and climbing, he would stalk German fighters who had not seen him; a 2 second kick of guns, a touch of rudder, a look in the mirror to check that he was not himself in the middle of a gun sight, and a Me 109 would belch yellow and black, shudder and roll over, its pilot wrestling with the canopy. The German pilot would bale out, clearing his tail-fin, and drop earthwards to fight again, perhaps even later that day. Fifty per cent of Luftwaffe pilots who were shot down lived to do just that – until the next time.

And no sooner had the dogfight started than it would all be over. Bursting through the cloud cover, fingers wrapped tight around trigger and throttle, stick locked first against the firewall to dive, then pulled tight into his groin to climb, the Mustang pilot would sail into clear air – and nothing. The sky would be deserted and, getting his breath back, he would regain radio contact with the rest of the group, his gun cameras loaded with the evidence of what had occurred in a flash of fire and reflexes. Another 4 hours to go before coffee and a cigarette back in his East Anglian mess – assuming that his plane was still fit to fly the distance.

The Mustang was earmarked for yet another novel air strategy. Nicknamed 'rhubarbing', this was the highly perilous business of strafing ground targets, usually airfields and German railway engines, on the way home. Although losses well in excess of those being suffered by the Americans had been inflicted on the Luftwaffe in the air, German fighter strength remained a cause for Allied concern. Speer's factories, cleverly dispersed around the Reich to make them more difficult to bomb, were turning planes out by the thousand: as many as three thousand a month were being built. The Germans were also introducing newer and better models, most significantly the Me 163 rocket plane and the Me 262 jet fighter, each of which could outfly the Mustang by over 100 miles (160 kilometres) an hour.

Lieutenant-General James Doolittle of the USAF refused to be complacent. He was convinced that the Germans still had it in their power to mount vast aerial defensive strikes. His doomsday scenario saw 2000 German fighters being put into the air in one huge 'big wing' which would destroy as many as a hundred American bombers. Goering, perhaps in desperation, was even more ambitious. He had set his sights on nothing less than destroying a thousand enemy bombers. Doolittle resolved to pre-empt his nightmare. First, he would quadruple the number of escort fighters from one for every two bombers to two for every one. And second, he was going to destroy the Luftwaffe – on the ground. Once again, the fighters would have to do it.

To provide the necessary incentive for what was to become the Mustang's riskiest form of combat – zero-altitude ground attacks on heavily defended installations – the Americans decided to give planes destroyed on the ground the same status as those shot down in the air. One successful strafe of a line of parked fighters might in theory qualify a rookie pilot for the rank of 'ace' in a few deadly seconds, albeit against sitting targets. In practice, most Mustang pilots used different insignia on the side of their cockpits to record ground and air victories.

Flying six miles up, a formation of Mustangs somewhere over Europe. With a range of over 1300 miles, they flew further than almost any other single-engined fighter in the war. On the return leg back from their targets, they would swoop down to almost zero altitude and attack targets on the ground.

Ground-level attacks, especially on heavily defended airfields, were particularly hazardous and accounted for the largest number of Mustang casualties. Turning back from Berlin, Magdeburg or Bremen, the crews of the Mustangs (alongside those of Lightnings and Thunderbolts) would keep their eyes peeled for 'targets of opportunity' – the distinctive shapes of German air bases, the triangle of runways and taxiing aprons lined with hangars and barracks. Dropping down from 30 000 feet (9100 metres) to tree level, the group would split into flights of up to eight aircraft, fan out over the surrounding countryside, and sweep in low and hard. Flying eight abreast, they would have at most two stabs at a target before the alerted defences zeroed in on them making any further attacks suicidal. Once a pilot had breached the ring of anti-aircraft fire, his job was the brutally simple one of raking the sitting targets with machine-gun fire, and avoiding the resulting explosions. Tankers would detonate, grounded fighters get shredded, aircraft personnel were mown down. The damage done to munitions and morale was significant.

From the air base, great arches of coloured flak, wild and wide to start with, would find the range and speed of the Mustangs, piercing the smoke shrouding the field and seeking out the marauding attackers. In this kind of attack a couple of rounds hitting the wing, which would cause minor damage at 30 000 feet (9100 metres), would be enough to knock a plane off balance, its wing tips or propeller clipping the ground, instantly converting it into a fireball ploughing into the earth.

Ground attack against the German train system was less risky. Following railway lines across the landscape, Mustangs would sooner or later encounter steaming railway engines. Unable to fire back, or change direction, these offered satisfying targets of real strategic significance. Without rolling stock, Germany's ability to transport reinforcements to help stem the Allied invasion in Normandy was severely crippled. In the early days after the beachhead was established on 6 June 1944, when success or failure lay crucially in the balance, this was of incalculable value to the Allies. So, too, was the fact that the Allied destruction of German aircraft was so great that the Luftwaffe had only 300 serviceable fighters with which to harry the beachhead – against a force of nearly 12 000 Allied planes. It was even worse on the Eastern Front where the Luftwaffe could pit only 500 fighters against a revitalized Soviet Air Force of 13 000 aircraft. It is no exaggeration to say that the Mustang – alongside the Thunderbolt and RAF Spitfires and Typhoons – played a decisive role in ensuring the success of the invasion.

It was the Mustang's increasing success escorting bombers that was to seal the fate of the German fatherland. The Luftwaffe's final defensive efforts were made in 1944, two in July and four in November, before losses forced them to disperse their remaining fighters over what remained of the Reich. The Mustang had established domination of the air over Germany.

A typical late 1944 raid followed a well-established pattern. Bombers would converge on a target such as Hanover or Regensburg. Up to four hundred German fighters would rise to meet them and, with losses rarely above low double figures, the Mustangs would destroy up to a quarter of the attacking interceptors. On 27 November 1944 a record 750 sorties were flown over southern and eastern Germany. By the end of the month a fifth of Germany's fighter force was irrevocably destroyed, half by the Mustangs alone, and it was obvious that American fears of a resurgent last stand by the Luftwaffe had been successfully forestalled. From December on, the Allies could safely claim total air supremacy. Far more dangerous to the lonely Mustang pilot, navigating, operating the plane and fighting, were accidents, malfunctions and the foul winter weather.

The Germans could now do little more than put up token, heroic resistance. In his classic book *Why the Allies Won*, Richard Overy quotes Luftwaffe general Adolf Galland who was forced to concede:

> *The ratio in which we fight today is about 1 to 7. The standard of the Americans is extraordinarily high. The day-fighters have lost more than 1000 aircraft during the last four months, among them our best officers. These gaps cannot be filled. Things have gone so far that the danger of a collapse of our arm exists.*

As another German air ace put it in a diary entry: 'It is a truly awe-inspiring spectacle which confronts us. There are approx. 1000 of the heavy bombers flying eastwards along a wide frontage with a strong fighter escort … Against them we are forty aircraft'. He, like Galland, was shot down by Mustangs a few months later, early in 1945.

Germany had lost the initiative and never regained it. The attack on the Luftwaffe had been intensified during the so-called 'big week' attack on German plane and engine plants. The already over-stretched aircraft factories were forced yet again to disperse their operations, making it impossible for them to meet the demand for 5000 new fighters a month. Most of these lasted only days: 9000 aircraft were destroyed on the ground without even taking off. By late 1944, an even more effective seal had been put on the Luftwaffe when Allied bombers turned their attention to the Rumanian oilfields as well as the synthetic-oil-production plants in Germany. Without fuel, even planes still in one piece were grounded. In January 1945 Albert Speer wrote to Hitler telling him the air war was effectively over.

The Mustang had transformed the air war overnight. Not only did the P-51s claim huge numbers of German fighters, they also helped to ensure the success of Allied bombing. They played a vital role in the defeat of Germany, not in any one single decisive encounter but in their unyielding whittling away of the German war machine. The Mustang was the fighter that took the battle to the Luftwaffe and destroyed it as a viable force, paving the way for D-Day and ensuring an unhindered advance from Normandy to Berlin. More even than this, it ensured that the bombers

could do their terrible work, destroying Germany's ability to fight the war.

The question of bombing is the most controversial issue – both morally and strategically – of post-war retrospect. The claim that it 'did not shorten the war by one day' has become a truism, while the fire storms of Hamburg and Dresden continue to haunt us as images of how even the just war sinks to barbarity. However, historians like Richard Overy have redressed the balance a little. He argues that, brutal and indiscriminate though much of the bombing was, there can be little doubt that a strategy that began merely for want of any other, developed into one of the key elements of Allied victory. Up to 1943, its effect was diminished by the casualty rate inflicted by German fighters, and lack of precision bombsight

Two ground crew inspect the Rolls-Royce Merlin engine that gave the Mustang its performance, stamina, and distinctive throaty roar. Another feeds the 50-calibre machine-guns with fresh ammunition belts. The Mustang had six of these guns, most effective at ranges of between 250 and 300 yards.

and target location technology. After 1943 it is a different story. The bombing of Germany paved the way for victory, and the Mustang helped that come about.

It came at a price: 140 000 Allied airmen were killed and 21 000 bombers destroyed. As a strategy bombing was expensive in lives but, because it absorbed only seven per cent of Britain's war effort, cheap for the exchequer. The figures are high but, as Overy shows, they are still far lower than those incurred by the land armies in the east. Destroying the Luftwaffe with bombs and fighters made D-Day possible and saved thousands of post-invasion casualties.

In short, the impact of bombing was decisive. Two and a half million tons of bombs not only pulverized vital communications and industrial targets (while also, undeniably, massacring huge numbers of civilians); they also forced the Germans to redeploy their resources from other fronts. The 55 000 anti-aircraft guns that fired curtains of flak at the B-17s had to come from somewhere – in this case the Eastern Front where they had been used as anti-tank guns against the advancing Red Army. Millions of front-line troops were denied to the Wehrmacht (the German Army) because they were needed to man the home air defences. Aircraft, too, were sucked back from the Russian Front for the defence of the homeland.

In production terms, too, the bombing forced Speer on to the defensive. First, he had to build fighters to protect Germany, rather than bombers to attack the Allied troops: by 1944 over 80 per cent of German planes were fighters built exclusively to defend the Reich. And second, he was prevented from successfully reaching his production targets. Numbers rose, it is true, but never enough. He was caught in a vicious circle as bombers destroyed the factories needed to produce the fighters that were shot down attacking the bombers.

The effect of the bombing on both the civilian and the working population was also dramatic. Like the British during the Blitz, the German civilians never capitulated even though they were bombed day and night – for every ton of bombs dropped on England, 14 were dropped on Germany. But they were browbeaten and traumatized by the experience and the effect on morale was pronounced. In the factories absenteeism was rampant and this, together with the lack of raw materials, increased the already deadly strain on Speer's factories. It is estimated that Allied bombs destroyed half of all the weapons produced for the German forces. Germany had been transformed from an impregnable fortress into a 'gigantic front', according to Albert Speer. When they lost this front, they lost the war and the nightmare was over.

The use of bombers was a strategy particularly suited to the Allies. In the beginning it was the only one they had against the German economic, territorial and military superpower. It played to an Allied strength that was not initially obvious, but which became decisive: America's superior industrial production. The story of the Mustang is not just a story of strategy, or even of the men who flew the plane. It is also about America, and its unique approach to war. Only the United States could have built the P-51; it emerged not just from the scale of the country's economy, but from something less tangible but nonetheless significant.

After a slow and shaky start, the American economy's real contribution to winning World War Two lay in its industrial capacity to mass-produce huge numbers of planes and weapons. But more than that, designers, engineers and managers in the United States rose to the challenge of conceiving, designing, selling – and then building in vast numbers – weapons that were as technically advanced and militarily effective as possible. The Mustang is the prime example of this, the product of a uniquely American initiative and will to win combined with technology married to derring-do.

THE MACHINE

THE MUSTANG MAY HAVE been an American plane, but it grew out of British requirements. As late as November 1939, the British Purchasing Committee (BPC) had scoured the United States in search of weapons to help shore up the European war. They desperately needed to reinforce the dwindling stock of British Hurricane and Spitfire fighters, and came to America to do just that.

While the Americans had been energetic in their development of powerful bombers, they had neglected the fighter. The Flying Fortress could fly faster than any contemporary American pursuit plane. Their best fighter was the ageing P-40 Curtiss Tomahawk (made famous by the Flying Tigers in China in the mid-1930s). Already lagging behind the best that the Germans could put in the air, it was nevertheless better than nothing. The British asked the Americans to commission a second Curtiss Wright plant to produce a version of the plane for them.

However, North American Aviation (NAA) had other, more ambitious, ideas. Why upgrade the old P-40 when you could have a new plane designed from scratch? The key question was not whether there was the will and the wherewithal to do this, but whether there was the time. Could a new plane be flying quickly enough to make its development worthwhile? It would take 120 days for the Curtiss Wright Corporation to produce a new version of the P-40; could NAA match that with a new fighter? NAA thought, yes, it could. The BPC agreed, and NAA assembled the design team for the first time on 24 April 1940, the eve of what was to become known as the Battle of Britain.

The BPC awarded the contract to NAA on 23 May at a unit price of $50 000. The British agreed to buy 320 of what was called the NA-73, as outlined by NAA's chief engineer, John Leland Atwood. Although this was only the company's second-ever venture into fighter production, the basic airframe development was completed in 102 days. Original drawings were produced by Raymond Rice, who had been NAA's chief engineer since 1939. The chief design engineer was German-born Edgar Schmued, and it was he who produced the first outlines of what was to become the P-51 for the rest of its career. 'P' is the American designation for a 'pursuit' plane, or fighter.

But what really set the initial design apart was its aerodynamic potential, the brainchild of another senior NAA designer, Edward Horkey. The first radical addition to the original specifications was to be the development of a laminar wing which promised far less drag than orthodox wings. Ever since June 1938 wind-tunnel tests on various aerofoil sections (wing shapes) had shown the advantages offered by a laminar design, though no production aircraft had as yet been

P-51 MUSTANG

It was, quite simply, the greatest single-engine fighter of the war. The Japanese Zero could fly further, the RAF Spitfire could climb faster, but only the P-51 could fly all the way to Berlin, beat the Luftwaffe, and fly back attacking ground targets on the way.

Although it was built by an American company, North American Aviation, the P-51 was originally commissioned for the British. It was the British, indeed, who christened the P-51, 'The Mustang' – a name that has stuck to this day.

It underwent a number of key modifications – most notably the introduction of a Rolls-Royce Merlin engine. This was much more powerful than its original Allison engine and doubled its altitude to 40 000 feet.

This later model Mustang has the distinctive tear-drop shaped canopy, and no dorsal fin. By 1945 their mastery of the skies over Germany was complete, and they would dispense with camouflage. The silver metal, and brightly painted noses, acted almost as a torment to the, by then beleaguered, Luftwaffe.

4 x Pratt and Whitney engines

Until 1943, German fighters ruled the skies over Germany

Armoured backrest

10 000 pounds of bombs

Aerial

Fin

Rudder

Trim

Elevator

D-Day stripes

Monocoque fuselage construction

Plexiglass bubble hood

Flap

Aileron

Powered gun turrets

B-17 flying fortress

On some raids as many as 60 planes would be lost

Focke-Wulf 190

With their 'Little Friends' there to escort them, American bombers were free to inflict massive damage to German factories and industrial infrastructure

Silver metal – by 1944 P-51s dispensed with camouflage

Gun sight

11'2" propeller

Rolls-Royce Merlin engine

Only the jet fighter the ME 262 could fly faster, but they were few in number and vulnerable to attack while taking off and landing.

Carburettor intake

Exhaust

Coolant system

Supercharger

Firewall

Laminar wing

Main spars

108 gallon paper/plastic composite drop-tank

3 x 50-calibre machine-guns

successfully fitted with this type of wing. The problem was that 'laminar flow' could be exploited only by perfectly smooth wings, impossible to achieve in a mass-produced fighter aircraft with its rivets, air ducts, ailerons and access handles. However, NAA engineers realized that it could be simulated, not perfectly, but well enough to produce a wing markedly superior to conventional ones.

The result was a 'No. 60' section, a wing whose main thickness was set as close to its rear as possible, two-thirds back from the leading edge. It did not eradicate the air turbulence that caused drag, but it minimized it. The result was one of the most sophisticated fighter wings produced in the war and accounted for the distinctive shape of the P-51, anticipating the next generation of jet fighters.

The aircraft would have the same Allison V-1710 engine as the Tomahawk, installed all the way back at the fire wall. The team's real genius, it is now obvious, lay in its ability to harness the latest aerodynamic research, wherever they could find it, and plough it back into the new design. This was where the Americans excelled, and the P-51 benefited enormously from the extensive research done by Curtiss in their bid to upgrade the Tomahawk.

This marriage of the practical and the theoretically cutting edge ensured that the new P-51 would be speedily completed – and also that it would be the most aerodynamically sophisticated fighter ever produced. It was the first aircraft whose contours were calculated with conic geometry, its lines constructed out of circles, parabolas and ellipses. This had two important consequences. Each curve in the airframe could be expressed algebraically, and every aspect of fuselage construction and layout could be easily controlled and mass-produced.

On 26 October 1940 test pilot Vance Breese took NX19998 – the codename for the NA-73 – into the air for its maiden flight from what is today Los Angeles airport. It was immediately obvious that it was a true original, a plane whose whole was greater than the sum of its parts. There were teething troubles, particularly with the positioning of the air duct, but the British were persuaded that this was an aircraft with a future. They placed an order for 300 more. They had initiated the NA-73, and it was they who were to christen it.

A popular tune at the time contained the line: 'Saddle your blues to a wild mustang and gallop your troubles away, away.' The BPC was struck by its aptness and on 9 December 1940 wrote to NAA instructing them to name the aircraft 'Mustang'.

The first Mustangs arrived in England for combat trials. Although its abilities at low and medium altitude were impressive, there was no hiding the fact that the Allison engine was a disappointment. The P-51 could dive, turn, climb and achieve an acceptable level flying speed, but not much more. Another problem was immediately apparent to the battle-scarred British observers. From underneath, the Mustang was the spitting image of the Me 109, sharing the German fighter's square wing outline. Frantic briefings went out to all Allied flak units. But before the war was over, many Mustangs were to fall victim to overzealous gunners mistaking them for Me 109s.

By April 1942 the Mustang was in active service, initially in a ground attack and reconnaissance role, to which it seemed particularly suited. It had its baptism of fire attacking petroleum depots in the Ruhr valley. By August the Mustang had had its first taste of aerial combat when four squadrons lent support to Typhoons and Spitfires in fierce action over Dieppe against some of the most concentrated formations of Luftwaffe fighters since the Battle of Britain.

So far so good. The Mustang was a well-liked addition to the Allied air arsenal, but it was the British who instigated a further transformation – from run-of-the mill fighter into perhaps the best pursuit plane of the war. The RAF was in any case quicker to see its potential than the USAF and was operating six squadrons of the aircraft by May 1942.

Ronald Harker, a Rolls-Royce test pilot, saw instantly that the reason why the Mustang promised more than it delivered was that it deserved a better engine, one that was the equal of its revolutionary fuselage and wing shape: the Merlin. Rolls-Royce, who produced this peerless engine (already powering the Spitfire fighter and the Lancaster bomber) were not initially very keen. But the RAF needed a fighter that was superior to the new generation FW 190s then spearheading the Luftwaffe's defence squadrons, and gave the go-ahead to marry the Mustang and the Merlin.

The Americans, too, realized that this was the advance the Mustang needed and set about equipping the aircraft with the Packard version of the Merlin, built under licence from Rolls-Royce in Detroit. The new P-51 needed considerable modifications to accommodate the bigger, more powerful and more temperamental engine. Finally, with a four-blade propeller to deal with the extra thrust, the new Mustang took to the air. With its distinctive spluttering roar, its superb engineering and its much-improved power and performance, the new engine was perfect for the Mustang, guaranteeing it a presence in the air unequalled by any other piston-engined fighter. By 1943 the P-51A and P-51B were familiar sights in the skies above Europe. The earlier models were followed by even better versions, most significantly the P-51D with its new and very distinctive bubble canopy and no long dorsal fin.

At precisely this moment in the Mustang's story it took advantage of another, crucial technological advance that would enable it to fulfil its role in World War Two. Although the 75 gallon (340 litre) external fuel tank was initially made out of reinforced paper, and rudely ditched at the first sign of trouble, it deserves to be recognized as a decisive weapon in its own right. It had been fitted to the Thunderbolt in an attempt to give the great 'Jug' a useful range, but it was the Mustang that really stood to exploit it.

Even without an external drop tank, the P-51 was so well geared that it could fly 600 miles (965 kilometres). With one, it could more than double this. The

Mustang used 64 gallons (290 litres) an hour, versus 144 gallons (655 litres) an hour burned up by the two-engined Lightning, and 140 gallons (635 litres) an hour by the Thunderbolt. It could carry enough fuel for 4¾ hours and needed a further reserve of only 100 gallons (455 litres) to make the 6 hour flight to Berlin and back, with enough over the target for air combat as well as 'rhubarbing' ground attacks all the way home.

The obvious tactic of the Luftwaffe would have been to engage the Mustangs as early as possible, crossing the coast on the way to their bomber rendezvous. Even if they had avoided being shot down, the Mustangs would have been forced to jettison their tanks while still full. This would have severely limited their subsequent range. However, the Germans adopted a different strategy. As the noose tightened, they withdrew their fighters deeper and deeper into Nazi heartland. The Americans looked on in grateful amazement. It was to be a fatal error. From that moment on, the Luftwaffe's days were numbered. Only now, safe in the knowledge that with their tanks intact, the Mustangs were being allowed to escort the bombers all the way to their targets, could General Kepner decide to allow his fighters to seek out the opposing German fighters, rather than just wait for them to attack the bombers. From now on, the Mustangs provided more than just a protective shield around the bombers, but became an offensive weapon of enormous power in their own right. As soon as their escort duties were discharged, the Mustangs could now come into their own as fighters. This suited their confident, ambitious young pilots only too well, eager as they were to engage the enemy.

The arrival of the Mustang, equipped with drop tanks, was in some ways nothing more than a lucky coincidence. As the 8th Air Force probed deeper and deeper into Fortress Europe, and was torn to shreds, it woke up to the need for long-range escorts – and needed them immediately. There was no time to build them from scratch. It did not have far to look and 13 December 1943 saw the first large-scale Mustang escort operation, in a bombing run over the northern port of Kiel. The fighters accompanied the 1462 bombers that took off all the way there and all the way back. This was the war the Mustang was going to win for the Allies. 'One of the great "miracles" of the war was the fact that the long range Mustang fighter escort did appear over Germany at just the saving moment,' said General 'Hap' Arnold.

The bomber pilots called their Mustang escorts 'Little Friends'. Early losses of daylight bombers were so heavy, the Americans almost considered stopping. It was fighters like the Mustang, able to provide escort all the way to the target and back, that allowed the Americans to continue their bombing.

THE VERDICT

UNTIL LATE 1943 the Mustang, in common with other American fighters, was camouflaged in standard olive green. This was later abandoned, both to save time in production and to increase speed by reducing drag. Perhaps it was also a gesture of chutzpah: by 1944 these shining silver fighters had no need to hide behind camouflage. They could flaunt their supremacy. And this is how the Mustang will always be remembered. It is in this silver guise that it set iself apart from the other fighters with which it flew. Perhaps only the Spitfire enjoys a higher reputation because of the quality of its lines and the impact of its appearance – compounded by the fact it won its legendary status at the beginning of the war in the teeth of near-certain defeat. The Mustang came to war late, but it provided the *coup de grâce*. With its prolonged snout, angled canopy, rear-sloping lines and square-tipped wings rakishly cut into the fuselage it was an aircraft that achieved what only a few machines can ever do (and which from a strictly military point of view is entirely superfluous): it became glamorous.

But the Mustang's glitter does not make it a decisive weapon. What makes it so is that it was instrumental in shaping one of the war's key strategic chapters: the defeat of Nazi Germany through daylight bombing. It not only enabled the bombers to do their job, but doubled the impact of the bombs by destroying the Luftwaffe in the air and on home soil. It was a brilliant act of faith, the bringing together in one aircraft of all the very best research and innovation at America's disposal, motivated by an extraordinary and gung-ho readiness to do whatever was necessary to conceive, produce and then fight with, the weapons that were needed to win the war.

It arrived on the battlefield at precisely the right time, able to adapt in an unforeseen way to meet unforeseen needs and excel in fulfilling them. Plenty of other fighters could nearly do the same job, and did so with distinction. But the Mustang had something extra, a kind of technological and historical charisma shared by very few other aircraft. Certainly, it looked the part; but more than that it was impossible to imagine an aircraft, in the hands of the men who flew it, using the available technology better.

History is written by the victors, and victorious planes become mythic, just as the FW 190 would have done if Germany had won. It is arguable that the Mustang had a short cut to fame, coming as it did at the end of the war when the Germans were beginning to wilt. But its battles, victories and defeats were real enough. It is easy now to think the Allied victory was simply a matter of time and superior American technological might. But that is not how it felt in 1943. The Mustang represented just one part of the transformation of the United States from the insular under-militarized nation it had been in 1940, to the global superpower it had become by 1945.

More than any other American fighter, the Mustang came to symbolize a force that enjoyed overwhelming technical and numerical superiority in the just war the Allies fought against Nazi barbarism. Little wonder that an element of moral superiority would rub off on it too. Compared to the ambiguities of later American military might, this was a simple war which the Mustang helped to win. It was a righteous plane in the days when such a thing was possible. Technologically, too, it offered the final word. Together with the Flying Fortresses and Liberators of the 8th Air Force, it formed part of the most powerful weapon yet produced: the escorted bomber force, able to raze cities at will, realizing H. G. Wells's apocalyptic 1908 vision that Armageddon would take the form of bombs falling out of the sky. The Mustang's superiority was, of course, short-term. The arrival of the jet and, even more potently, the atom bomb meant that the P-51 – alongside the Flying Fortress – would quickly fall by the wayside, to be replaced by even deadlier combinations of speed, agility and explosive yield. But between the spring of 1944 and the summer of 1945, the Mustang was truly a decisive weapon.

CHAPTER 5

THE BELL 'HUEY' UH-1 HELICOPTER

Speed and flexibility are the hallmarks of the airmobile division. They are the equalizers that overcome the lack of heavy groundborne weapons.

ARMY MAGAZINE, AUGUST 1965

You can kill ten of my men for every one that I kill of yours. But even at those odds, you will lose and I will win.

HO CHI MINH,
PRESIDENT OF NORTH VIETNAM, 1946

THE CHALLENGE

VIETNAM IS A WILDERNESS of mirrors.

Even our memory of the war, after years of intensive soul-searching in books, films and documentaries, is jumpy and freaked, hyped on the adrenaline infusion of rampant technology, kill-ratios, and grainy television images: a jungle fever born out of the collision of the ideals of a young and unquestioning army with the reality of what war in Vietnam was really all about.

It is appropriate that when you stand at the Vietnam memorial in Washington DC and gaze at the roll call of the dead carved into that black obsidian surface, what you see is your own reflection broken and refracted by those 58 169 names. A generation is tattooed with the memory of this war.

Vietnam causes pain and passion because, for the United States, it was a turning, or breaking, point. And what breaks in the United States in the second half of the twentieth century breaks for much of the rest of the world as well. The fall-out has been immense; it has done nothing less than redefine the way in which the 'developed' world has perceived, traded with, defined, policed and intervened in the so-called 'third world'. Militarily, it has restructured thinking in terms of strategy, tactics and technology. The 1991 Gulf War, to take an obvious example, was fought as one long good-bye to the military mistakes of Vietnam. 'By God, we've kicked the Vietnam syndrome once and for all,' said United States president George Bush in a moment of post-war exhilaration.

In the Gulf War the dark, dripping confusion of 'Nam had seemingly been exchanged for the surgical precision of hi-tech desert fighting (before we learned that many Iraqi soldiers had been buried alive in trenches). On the symbolic level, at least, Vietnam's ghosts had been pushed a bit further back into the dark corners of the mind.

Central to the story of what happened in Vietnam is the helicopter, especially the UH-1 or, as the army – the 'grunts on the ground' – preferred to call it, the 'Huey'. It sums up much of what the war was about: belief in technology versus nationalistic pride; 'search and destroy' versus infiltration; American troops literally flown into battle versus soldiers on foot. And it was also about the United States military's belief in their ability to 'find them, fuck them and forget them' versus the Vietnamese strategy of 'clinging to the belt'.

PREVIOUS SPREAD: *The helicopter transformed war. Now troops could be dropped at landing zones far from their original base. This transformed the way the American generals thought about Vietnam. Difficult terrain was no longer a hindrance to rapid response.*

The US Army of 1965, and more specifically the 1st Cavalry Division (Airmobile) which was airlifted into the jungle of the Ia Drang valley in October that year, was a product of intensive training as well as years of strategic thought and analysis. These were prime troops, honed and trained for a new kind of warfare. The thrust behind airmobility, as this new concept of fighting was called, has it roots in the army's attempt to forge a new identity in the early 1960s, the years immediately following Dwight Eisenhower's administration. Eisenhower had believed in massive nuclear retaliation. During his presidency military thought and planning had reduced the army's contribution to a projected third world war to 'occupying the radioactive rubble of Eastern Europe, Russia and China' after the air force and the navy had won the hypothetical battle by unleashing their thermonuclear missiles from planes and submarines. As Neil Sheehan points out in his wide-ranging and important book on Vietnam, *A Bright Shining Lie*, the army was out to redefine its mission and its identity in the new climate of John F. Kennedy's administration.

Kennedy used the language of war to define America's role in the struggle with the perceived communist threat. During his inaugural address on 20 January 1961 he pledged that the United States would 'pay any price, bear any burden, meet any hardship, support any friend, oppose any foe, to assure the survival and the success of liberty'. And to back up his public eloquence he set about creating a military that would draw upon the latest thinking and tactics in weapons and mobility. The army was key to this concept; Maxwell Taylor, a highly respected general and Kennedy's military adviser, was to forge it into a mobile and effective weapon to be used in the strategy of 'flexible response'. This was the muscle in the new way of thinking about war: instead of the all-or-nothing option of massive and overwhelming nuclear assault, Taylor's belief in the effectiveness of 'limited war' provided the general context in which specific doctrines such as airmobility – the prized offspring of the union between the army, struggling to redefine itself, and the new technology of the helicopter – were formed.

In 1961, during a visit to Southeast Asia, Taylor realized that South Vietnam's lack of an adequate road network, poor lines of communication, and the physical difficulties involved in getting from one part of the country to another helped to explain the military problems the Republic of Vietnam was experiencing in its fight against the communist-directed Vietcong from the north.

President Kennedy approved a more active support programme for South Vietnam – his administration was called 'Camelot' for its self-conscious heroism and chivalric spirit, and his attitude to Vietnam could be paraphrased from the contemporary Broadway musical *Camelot* as a belief in 'might in the cause of right' – and began a chain of events that resulted in the first army aviation units arriving in Vietnam in December 1961. These comprised one fixed-wing unit and three H-21 companies, each consisting of 32 helicopters and 400 men, to be used in an 'advisory' role. These precursors to the UH-1 Huey, called 'flying bananas', were involved in Operation Chopper, the first airmobility combat action in Vietnam, on 23 December 1961. Its objective was to seek out a Vietcong radio transmitter. The mission was successful in terms of moving troops, but its goal proved elusive. No radio transmitter was found.

In Washington, moves were afoot that would have a major impact on the future of airmobility and the helicopter's role in war. In January and February 1962 US Secretary of Defence Robert McNamara, the technocratic whiz kid from the Ford Motor Corporation, set his advisers on to the army's plans for airmobility. They turned in a ferociously critical report and on 19 June McNamara sent a memo to Elvis Stahr, the secretary of the army, in which he claimed that the airmobility programme was dangerously conservative and that the opportunities of the new technology had not been fully seized upon or explored. He strongly suggested that the army re-examine its aviation requirements and take a bold 'new look' at land warfare mobility.

The army reacted swiftly. Within a week of receiving McNamara's memo, they appointed a board of 13 general officers and five senior civilians headed by General Hamilton Howze, commander of the 17th Airborne Corps stationed at Fort Bragg, North Carolina. He was appointed to conduct a thorough re-examination of the role of army airmobility and aircraft requirements as president of the US Army Tactical Mobility Requirements Board.

The Howze board, as it became known, undertook approximately 40 tests. They included elaborate live-fire exercises, and three major week-long exercises against assumed forces which showed the desirability of using helicopters in both conventional war scenarios and in counter-guerrilla operations; they would, in the language of the military, 'enhance combat effectiveness'. On 20 August 1962, the board submitted its suggestions which included the formation of an air assault division of 459 aircraft and an air cavalry combat brigade with 316 aircraft, 144 of which would be attack helicopters.

The function of the air cavalry, like that of any cavalry, would be to screen, reconnoitre, and wage delaying actions. The board's single major conclusion was emphatic: 'Adoption by the Army of the airmobility concept – however imperfectly it may be described and justified in this report – is necessary and desirable. In some respects the transition is inevitable, just as was that from animal mobility to motor transport.' As Sheehan points out, the air cavalry was the next move forward in mobility, just as the jeep and truck divisions of World War Two and Korea had taken over from previous cavalry traditions of horse and mule. The Howze board had completed its mission in just 90 days from original assignment to final report.

The next stage was to implement its findings. McNamara liked what he saw but was hesitant about the cost of putting the plans into action. The 11th Air Assault

Division (Test) was created on 15 February 1963 at Fort Benning, Georgia, to try out the concept before committing serious money. A parachute officer, Brigadier General Harry Kinnard, was given its command.

Kinnard was a veteran of World War Two who had made his reputation as an airborne commander and a staff officer and who had written a paper in 1950 outlining his thoughts on the tactical use of the helicopter. He was the right man for the job. At about this time the army began receiving the Bell UH-1D which could carry 12 to 14 troops. The smaller UH-1B which entered service in March 1964 held seven men but, more important, it could be armed with .30-calibre machine-guns and up to forty-eight 2¾-inch rockets.

Throughout 1963 and into 1964 the air assault division trained its ground and air elements together to create a well-organized and co-ordinated combat team. The summer of 1964 was spent preparing for tests in the Carolinas. The main thrust of these was still towards medium- or high-intensity combat environments rather than counterinsurgency: the military is a traditional institution and its commanders, especially those like General William Westmoreland, were modelling future conflicts on the examples of World War Two and even the American Civil

This Huey, its blades still turning, has flown in to pick up the wounded. This chopper is a medi-vac. The Huey was originally conceived as a flying ambulance but its potential fighting capabilities, especially in jungle environments, proved decisive.

War. Although 'flexible response' was being discussed, the division artillery at one time boasted a Little John rocket battalion with battlefield nuclear weapon capability. Flexible or not, the military liked to know it had the ability to deliver the ultimate big punch to the enemy.

The final test, held on 14 October 1964, was the largest manoeuvre held in the United States since World War Two. Over the next 30 days the theory of airmobility received its ultimate challenge in a series of exercises held over 6000 square miles (15 540 square kilometres) of the Carolinas. The 82nd Airborne Division and tank and mechanized battalions of the 2nd Infantry Division played the aggressor forces.

The helicopters were able to outmanoeuvre armoured divisions, strike at the rear of the aggressor forces, move battalions rapidly, provide crucial logistical support ('beans and bullets') and were effective scouts in enemy territory. Although it was recognized that air assault had limitations, especially in prolonged fighting, its capacity for rapid reaction was overwhelming.

By 1965 the problems in Vietnam, which had been simmering since the end of World War Two, were vaster and more pressing. The United States had been propping up the government in the south since 1961 but a series of coups – there were seven in 1964 – had left it looking shaky and unstable. The Central Intelligence Agency (CIA) had estimated that up to 100 000 communist North Vietnamese guerrillas were infiltrating South Vietnam. These Vietcong fighters symbolized the red scare, the deeply held American fear that communism would overrun Vietnam, resulting in the 'domino effect' of other Southeast Asian countries falling to the spectre of this much feared ideology. In addition, there were reports that divisions of the people's army regulars were moving down from the north to join in the struggle. The United States would have to intervene with significant force in order to prevent the defeat of South Vietnam and the Army of the Republic of Vietnam (ARVN).

1965 saw the first major move in the escalation of the war, the first pledge of troops in what became a seemingly inescapable series of steps that resulted in the country's commitment to a war that no one back home ever really understood. (The United States' previous commitment had been in the form of a more delicate and mincing trickle of military advisers and materials.)

Sustained strikes against North Vietnam started on 19 February 1965 but the brunt of the bombing began on 2 March. Over one hundred aircraft were launched from aircraft-carriers in the South China Sea and air bases in South Vietnam. This was the start of Operation Rolling Thunder, and the noise and smoke and bombs of this campaign would continue to roll over Vietnam for another three years. 'We are going to stomp them to death,' said a brigadier general at its start.

The human dimension was added to the war at 09:03 on 8 March 1965 as the first US marines came ashore at Red Beach 2, a few miles north-west of Da Nang.

Their initial mission was defensive: they had ostensibly been sent to protect American aircraft and bases. But within a month President Johnson had authorized the use of ground combat troops to carry out offensive operations. There was no turning back.

On 16 June 1965, in a nationally televised address, McNamara announced the authorization of an airmobile division within the army's force structure. The 11th Air Assault Division was to take up the colours of the famous 1st Cavalry Division and would have eight weeks to reach REDCON 1 – the highest state of combat readiness. Brigadier General Kinnard was chosen to lead the new division.

The cavalry spirit had already been adopted with great gusto by Lieutenant-Colonel John Stockton (the *Apocalypse Now* commander who loves 'the smell of napalm in the morning' was roughly modelled on him). He sported the handlebar moustache of the old-time cavalryman and all his men had to do the same. He ordered black cavalry hats for everyone in the squadron and made wearing them mandatory on special occasions. His officers had to wear the crossed sabres of the cavalry. When the colours of the 11th Air Assault Division were ceremonially retired, it was Stockton, dressed in the uniform of a 1930s cavalryman and mounted on a cavalry charger, who took up those of the 1st Cavalry Division to the strains of the regimental song 'Garryowen'. In July 1965 he assumed command of the only true air cavalry formation within the 1st Cavalry – the 1st of the 9th.

Communist attacks had concentrated on South Vietnamese units during June that year. The Vietcong were rapidly annihilating the ARVN who were losing the equivalent of a battalion a week in battle. Johnson felt he had to commit more troops and on 26 June General Westmoreland, Commander MACV (US military assistance in Vietnam) received permission to use his forces for offensive operations. On 1 July another contingent of marines landed at Qui Nhon.

Regiments of the North Vietnamese Army (NVA) had moved down the Ho Chi Minh trail into the Central Highlands from neighbouring Cambodia. The NVA was keen to engage the American troops in a direct battle in an attempt to see how they fought and what the best tactical response might be.

On 28 July 1965, in a television address to the nation, President Johnson described the worsening situation in Vietnam. As a result of 'the lessons of history' he had decided to launch a major military intervention there. And in the midst of his speech, he declared: 'I have today ordered to Vietnam the airmobile division …'

Commitment to a full-scale war in Vietnam had been announced and, along with it, the launch of the 1st Cavalry Division (Airmobile). Airmobility was identified with the prosecution of the war: new tactics to meet the communist threat in Southeast Asia. As such, the story of airmobility and the Huey is also the story of Vietnam. From the start, it served as a parable for the lessons of the war.

The division was shipped across the Pacific on 15 August 1965. Its ultimate destination was a base in the Central Highlands at An Khe where the world's largest helipad – known as the 'golf course' – was cleared out of the undergrowth of the jungle. In just 104 days, the new air cavalry division had achieved combat readiness. It had moved its men and its machines over 12 000 miles (19 300 kilometres) – a phenomenal feat of logistics and organization.

The 66th Regiment of the North Vietnamese Army (NVA) set off down the Ho Chi Minh trail in the week that the 1st Cavalry Division shipped out to meet up with two other regiments, the 33rd and 320th, at a base on the eastern slopes of the Chu Pong massif, a massive outcrop that straddled Vietnam's border with Cambodia. The NVA's intention was to lure the United States troops into a fight. It had first encountered American helicopters in 1962 when counterinsurgency specialist Roger Hilsman had enthusiastically reported that the aircraft were such a 'terrifying sight to the superstitious Vietcong peasants' that they easily flushed them from cover and shot them down as they fled. But this was a significant misreading of what was actually the simple panic of raw troops facing a new weapon. Even then, the Vietcong were developing new tactics to deal with the helicopter, as they showed at Ap Bac in January 1963 when they defeated a major drive by the ARVN. The battle of Ia Drang between the NVA and American troops, would give them another opportunity to refine their thoughts and actions.

The precursor to the battle occurred when an ARVN armoured column from Pleiku City was ambushed by the NVA in the late evening of 19 October even though there was air cover from the 1st Cavalry. The NVA regulars were aiming to

seize Pleiku province and establish control of the plateau in the hope of staging an eventual thrust to the coast, thus splitting Vietnam in two. It was six long days before the South Vietnamese troops and the American green berets at Plei Me, who were there to lend back-up support, were relieved and the NVA was driven back. Brigadier General Kinnard met General Westmoreland who had previously, over Kinnard's successful objections, wanted to break up the new helicopter division. Kinnard was anxious to show what his troops and machines could do; he argued that he wanted to do more than support the ARVN or contain the enemy. He wanted to seek out and destroy the NVA. Westmoreland was eventually persuaded to 'give Kinnard his head'.

THE BATTLE

IA DRANG, THE US ARMY'S first battle in Vietnam, was fought in the valley of the Ia (River) Drang and was in fact a series of engagements between the US 1st Cavalry Division (Airmobile) and the NVA's 66th, 33rd and 320th regiments. It lasted from 19 October to 25 November 1965 and may have been the first and last battle fought between United States and North Vietnamese forces of equivalent size.

A search for the NVA forces involved in the attack on Plei Me was undertaken by the 1st Squadron, 9th Cavalry led by Lieutenant-Colonel John Stockton. It consisted of 1000 men and 88 helicopters in five company-sized troops: headquarters; A; B; C (aerial reconnaissance); and D (motorized reconnaissance). Each troop was made up of a headquarters platoon, a scout platoon (white), a gunship platoon (red) and an infantry platoon (blue). Red, white and blue: the colours of the American flag.

Stockton decided to move three air troops to a base south of Pleiku City and they started the operation by searching to the east, west and south of Plei Me – army intelligence had no way of knowing which way the enemy forces had gone once they had broken camp.

Scout pilots (white) flew at tree-top level and were protected by the gunships (red) which flew in low orbits over them. This formation, called 'recon by decoy',

The Air Cavalry was the technological offspring of General Custer's horse cavalry in the 19th century. Its job was to reconnoitre and engage the enemy with speed and agility. Some of the Huey pilots took the cavalry roots seriously and wore the traditional insignia on their uniforms.

was a dangerous but effective method for drawing out the enemy: if the North Vietnamese fired at one of the lone and fragile-looking scout helicopters they would immediately be hit by rocket and machine-gun fire from the powerful gunships circling behind and overhead. On the first run, a gunship would fly in 'hot' and deliver bursts of fire from its machine-guns. It would then pull up in a steep, banking motion, like a sideways skid through the air, which would give the door gunners a clearer shot at the target. They fired M-60 machine-guns slung from heavy elastic cords attached to the roof of the Huey. In effect, they had 'retro-fitted' the helicopters with the necessary lethal equipment. If there seemed to be some kick in the enemy's fire and strength the blue platoon of infantry might be airlifted into the battle.

The cavalry helicopters searched fruitlessly for the enemy during the 30th and 31st October. On 1 November a team of scout helicopters and its accompanying gunship spotted soldiers in the jungle 8 miles (13 kilometres) west of Plei Me. Stockton ordered the blue infantry into the area and they were soon advancing on what turned out to be the field hospital of the NVA's 33rd Regiment. Within 30 minutes they had captured the hospital and had taken 44 prisoners. Fifteen of the enemy were killed and about a hundred escaped. The Americans had no casualties and took over the hospital, as well as all the NVA's supplies of rice and weapons. Enemy documents showing maps of the area were discovered. The engagement was a success.

One of the maps was of the Ia Drang valley and showed the trails the North Vietnamese were using to cross from Cambodia into Vietnam and group together in the secret base at Chu Pong mountain. On 3 November Stockton began a reconnaissance of one of the trails. It was a prime example of helicopter mobility – the logistics involved moving troops a huge distance from their fixed base, a thrust deep into the jungle which conventional forces would not have been able to accomplish either as effectively or as quickly. An advance party chose a spot called landing zone (LZ) Betty and the troops were flown in.

Stockton sent out three platoons, one of which successfully ambushed an NVA company at night as it passed on the trail. Captain Charles S. Knowlen of the ambush platoon then ordered his men to return to base; he did not realize that vestiges of the decimated NVA company were tracking them back to LZ Betty. Within half an hour the perimeter of the landing zone was under heavy attack. The Americans would have been overrun had Stockton not helicoptered in reinforcements. Huey gunships 'maintained a ring of rocket fire around the perimeter bringing in fire as close as they dared,' Stockton recalled later. The small and fleet bubble H-13 scout helicopters were unscathed but the bigger Huey gunships, all 88 of them, were repeatedly hit by gunfire. Stockton had saved the lives of his men but by calling in reinforcements he had broken direct orders not to send in more troops without first receiving authorization. As a result, the maverick commander was relieved of his duty.

In retrospect, this engagement was a watershed in the use of helicopters in Vietnam. It lay down the template for what was to come later and initiated the first serious use of these aircraft in battle. It was the first time that an American ambush had been successful in a remote outpost far from a 'safe' base. It was also the first time that troops under attack at their perimeter had been reinforced by gunships that laid down protective fire at night. Although the Hueys had been hit by small-arms fire none was damaged beyond repair.

The ambush had been successful. However, the American military knew there were more NVA troops somewhere in the vicinity. General Westmoreland sent word through Kinnard, by now promoted to Major-General, that he wanted Colonel Thomas Brown to search west towards the Cambodian border. Brown was at a loss: he did not know exactly how far west he should search. So he went to 2 Corps intelligence headquarters looking for a lead.

He found one, in the haphazard and serendipitous way of many military encounters. While talking to an intelligence officer he noticed a red star on a briefing map that pointed to a huge and forbidding massif, a formation of peaks and ridges and outcrops that rose out of the Ia Drang valley. The intelligence officer confirmed that it was thought to be a secret Vietcong base but that no one had been there. It seemed a promising place for Brown to start. He ordered his battalion commander, Lieutenant-Colonel Harold Moore, to choose a landing zone and explore the area. The scene was set.

Moore received his orders on 13 November. On the North Vietnamese side, Brigadier General Chu Huy Man had withdrawn to his well-developed sanctuary in the Chu Pong massif to regroup and re-organize. The 320th and 33rd regiments of the people's army had been joined by the 66th. October and November had not been successful for the general. The earlier plan to drive a wedge of NVA soldiers across the country to the sea had been abandoned by Hanoi and his mission was now to learn how to fight American troops and their weapons. This strategy had already proved costly – his 33rd Regiment had lost 40 per cent of its men in combat.

The battlefield area covered 1500 square miles (3885 square kilometres) of flat, rolling terrain dominated by the Chu Pong massif. Much of the valley was covered with thick, jungle vegetation. Trees could grow as high as 100 feet (30.5 metres) and even in the more open areas jungle vegetation could reach 6 feet (1.8 metres). The valley was fed by a network of streams and rivers.

Moore would have 16 UH-1D Hueys to move his troops – Alpha, Bravo and Charlie companies – and two batteries of six howitzers within support range as well as aerial rocket artillery support. He would have two days on the ground. His first move was to take a reconnaissance flight and pick out the most desirable landing zones. He chose X-Ray, Tango and Yankee; X-Ray, at the foot of Chu Pong mountain, looked the most promising. On 14 November the area was given a once-over by the long-range artillery. The helicopters took off from their base at Plei Me and arrived over the landing zone just as the white phosphorus shells that dramatically signalled the end of the artillery preparation had burst. It was time to go in.

The landing routine was a synchronized mechanical ballet of violence. The aerial rocket artillery made two passes, firing into the perimeter surrounding the landing zone with rockets, grenades and machine-gun fire. They were followed by the 229th escort gunships which made rocket and machine-gun passes at the edge of the landing zone. They fired 24 of their 48 rockets and saved the rest in case the troops needed help after they hit the ground. Finally the lead choppers came in over the edge of the clearing, the gunners blasting away at the jungle. Given their thunderous entry, it is perhaps ironic that they landed without opposition.

Soon afterwards a platoon captured a lone Vietcong deserter who had been living on bananas for five days. He told Moore that three battalions of the NVA were in the recesses of Chu Pong and that they were actively looking forward to an engagement with American troops. Moore verified this information – an air cavalry scout helicopter had spotted a trail – and began to plan his response.

He was an adept and agile soldier. Sheehan, who flew into the battle of X-Ray as a reporter, depicts him as a passionate fighter, keen to beat the enemy and extremely loyal to his men. Moore was also clever: his quick thinking and daring tactics saved many lives at X-Ray. Once he had decided that the deserter was telling the truth he knew that he had a major fight on his hands. He was smack in the middle of a hornets' nest.

Moore directed all the firepower he could muster into the vicinity of LZ X-Ray and air and ground support was mobilized. He sent Bravo company up the ridge: they met the attacking NVA in the trees where the rain forest started. Alpha was left to secure the perimeter around the landing zone. This clearing in the jungle was the Americans' island of security. It was where the helicopters could land and it was therefore their key to supplies of troops and ammunition as well as their escape route if things got bad. It was, in other words, the staging point for the 'air bridge' back to base. If the enemy broke through the perimeter, or swept around and found a gap in the defence, the whole operation would end in disaster.

Moore's tactical thinking was brilliant. He foresaw that the NVA would try to surround Bravo company and to block that move he sent Alpha to its flank – once the landing zone was secure – to stop a flanking operation by the North Vietnamese. And as fast as the men of Charlie company came in, he sent them to protect Alpha's left side. They spotted the NVA sweeping around Alpha and called in Huey aerial-rocket attacks as well as artillery and did as much as they could with machine-guns on the ground. It was ferocious fighting.

The Bell 'Huey' was the work-horse of the Vietnam War. It was used as gunship, air-ambulance and troop-carrier, and saw service throughout the conflict.

Moore's pattern of deployment involved risk. By sending his men out in this way he was leaving the rear of the clearing unprotected. He was guessing that the NVA would not consider sending troops that far round in a flanking movement. If they did, they could shut down the landing zone with very little resistance.

Meanwhile, one overly eager second lieutenant, who had been sent up to the ridge, spotted what looked like some fleeing NVA soldiers and set off with his platoon to try to bring them down. The North Vietnamese led him away from the other American troops and he and his men were surrounded and cut off on the crest of the ridge. They were in a desperate position. The inexperienced second lieutenant had fallen for the classic Vietnamese technique of 'the lure'. Moore sent more men up to the ridge in an attempt to rescue the platoon but they made little progress: the fighting was fast and furious.

More men came into the landing zone by helicopter during the afternoon whenever conditions allowed them to – photographs show, in the words of Moore in *We Were Soldiers Once … And Young* which he wrote with Joseph Galloway, 'smoke boiling off the X-Ray battlefield'. Moore had lost the major clearing for the Hueys and was calling in heavy firepower: jet bombers, aerial rocket artillery and field artillery to open it up again. It was major technological warfare – the field artillery alone was arcing in from LZ Falcon about 5 miles (8 kilometres) away. Still the helicopters flew in, even under heavy fire. One pilot, Bruce Crandall, flew his Huey non-stop from 6 a.m. to 10 p.m. under some of the most intense and dangerous conditions of the engagement.

As the evening closed in, Moore pulled his troops back into the comparative safety of the perimeter. In Plei Me Colonel Brown had realized that the NVA were intent on annihilating Moore's forces and was preparing to send in yet more men and machines. Concern on the ground was focused on the platoon stranded on the ridge. Over the radio, it seemed that morale was holding up. Eight of the 27 men had been killed and 12 wounded; but they continued to hold off vicious NVA probes with machine-gun fire and artillery. Their survival was down to the clear-headed thinking and grit of Staff Sergeant Clyde Savage, only 22 years old, who called artillery fire in to an amazing 25 yards (23 metres) from their position. World War One had seen the advent of the creeping barrage, where soldiers tried to move forward behind a slowly advancing wall of falling artillery. This was a surrounding barrage: a defensive curtain of exploding shells that kept the NVA away from killing-range.

The Vietnamese continued to hurl men at the perimeter of the landing zone, especially to the south and south-east. During the previous day their commander, Senior Lieutenant-Colonel Nguyen Huu An, had been frustrated because his men had not fully encircled it. They were trying hard to make up for this during the night.

Charlie company had managed to avoid heavy fighting but their time came as dawn broke on Monday 15 November. Moore had ordered each of his platoon leaders to send men out to scout the position of the enemy; those from C company walked straight into North Vietnamese creeping towards them through the elephant grass. Some of them died in close fighting; others were shot down as they came out in an attempt to mount a rescue. The NVA saw that there was a chance to overrun C company and fought hard to break open the perimeter.

Moore refused C company's requests for more troops. He did not know where the next strike would come from and could not afford to drain all his men away to one area before he knew for certain where the NVA were concentrating their next attack. In a move that echoed Sergeant Savage's method of defence during the previous night, he ordered all his units to throw coloured smoke grenades and called in supporting fire right up to the edge of the perimeter. Air force, navy and marine fighter-bombers and Huey gunship pilots brought their vast firepower to bear on the jungle just outside the landing zone. Aircraft were stacked at 1000 foot (305 metre) intervals in a section of airspace that ascended from 7000 to 35 000 feet (2130 to 10 668 metres). The American forces had complete dominance in the air.

With so much artillery and bombs falling in such a limited area, the inevitable was bound to happen. In *We Were Soldiers Once … And Young* Moore describes how he was down on one knee, looking south at Chu Pong mountain, when a movement caught his eye. Coming straight at him, and at the nerve centre of his operations, were two American F-100 Super Sabre jet fighters. He watched in amazed horror as two 6 foot (1.8 metre) long canisters of napalm were released from the lead fighter and began their sickening descent towards his command post. The second plane was frantically called off before it too could release its deadly napalm. But the canisters did hit and men were badly burned. Joseph Galloway got to one charred soldier and grabbed his feet; his boots crumbled and the flesh of his ankles came off in Galloway's hands. A stack of M-16 ammunition 'cooked off' in a crazy firework-like orgy of explosions.

Meanwhile, Moore had decided to commit another platoon (the 1st battalion of the 7th Cavalry) to prevent the total destruction of C company. It was a tattered fighting unit by the time the assault had lost its push – of the 100 men who had seen dawn break that morning, only 40 were without wounds a few hours later. Both sides had fought hard: a second lieutenant was found dead in his foxhole with the bodies of five NVA men lying around him. And in the elephant grass, a North Vietnamese and an American soldier had shot each other and lay in a death-embrace. The American died with his hands around the throat of the Vietnamese.

That afternoon, the stranded platoon was rescued by forces which had marched from another landing zone 2 miles (3.2 kilometres) away. At dawn on Tuesday 16 November a third assault was launched by the NVA but the North Vietnamese were losing their punch. The Huey 'air bridge' had held and replacements were coming in. Moore would not leave the battlefield until he had located the bodies of three of his sergeants from C company, and delayed the final

The Bell 'Huey' UH-1 Helicopter

The Hueys were most famously flown by the 1st Air Cavalry. Their pilots modelled themselves on General Custer's Cavalry, wearing black stetson hats, with crossed sabre insignia, and using the old Irish drinking song 'Garryowen' as their regimental anthem. They were among the most gung-ho American soldiers who fought in Vietnam.

The Huey, however, misled the Americans into a false sense of security. The North Vietnamese would lure the American helicopters deeper and deeper into their terrain. 95 per cent of all battles in the Vietnam War were started by the North Vietnamese. Slowly but surely the Americans were being worn down. Suffering huge casualties and losing support at home, the war degenerated into a long drawn out nightmare. By 1975 the Americans had lost 58 000 casualties – while having killed 3 million Vietnamese, many of whom were civilians.

The helicopter came to war for the first time in Vietnam. A small 'bubble' helicopter had seen service in Korea, but only as an aerial ambulance. Vietnam became a helicopter war thanks to the Huey; simple to fly, robust, powerful and able to operate in the difficult terrain of Southeast Asia with its forests, mountains and jungle.

Tail rotor – to stop helicopter spinning and providing torque compensation thrust

48' blades

Drive shaft to tail rotor

Anti-collision lights

Tail rotor gearbox

Synchronized elevator

Landing zone

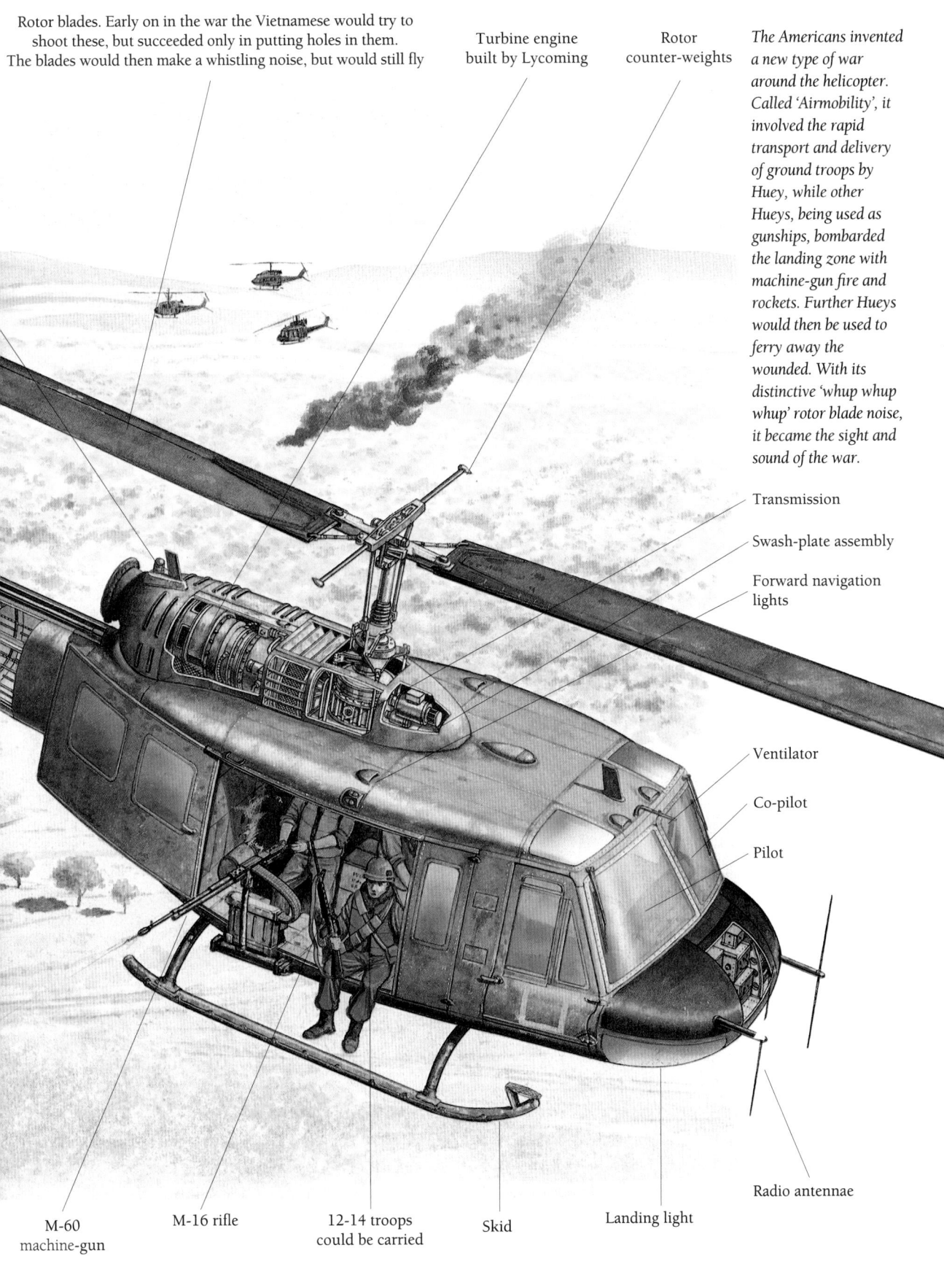

Rotor blades. Early on in the war the Vietnamese would try to shoot these, but succeeded only in putting holes in them. The blades would then make a whistling noise, but would still fly

Turbine engine built by Lycoming

Rotor counter-weights

The Americans invented a new type of war around the helicopter. Called 'Airmobility', it involved the rapid transport and delivery of ground troops by Huey, while other Hueys, being used as gunships, bombarded the landing zone with machine-gun fire and rockets. Further Hueys would then be used to ferry away the wounded. With its distinctive 'whup whup whup' rotor blade noise, it became the sight and sound of the war.

Transmission

Swash-plate assembly

Forward navigation lights

Ventilator

Co-pilot

Pilot

Radio antennae

M-60 machine-gun

M-16 rifle

12-14 troops could be carried

Skid

Landing light

movement of his troops out of X-Ray until he knew what had happened to all his men: he was adamant that he would not leave anyone behind. When everyone had been accounted for he pulled out and left the landing zone to the 2nd battalion, 7th Cavalry. He had not slept for 48 hours.

On Wednesday 17 November the 2nd battalion, 7th Cavalry, was ambushed while on the move from X-ray to LZ Albany. Senior Lieutenant-Colonel Nguyen Huu An had observed Moore's troops leaving the landing zone, but he did not feel that the fight was over. His concept of the battle was much more fluid: it was simply moving to a new location. The Americans were marching in a column and Nguyen ordered his battalions to '… move inside the column, grab them by the belt, and thus avoid casualties from the artillery and air.' The American battalion was enveloped in a U-shaped ambush: 151 soldiers were killed, 121 were wounded and four went missing in action. The North Vietnamese had sustained extremely high casualties at X-Ray but their commander was already learning the lessons of combating an airmobile army: get in close so that the advantage of the air is minimized.

THE MACHINE

THE 1ST CAVALRY DIVISION (Airmobile) had come formally into existence only some three months before the start of the battle of Ia Drang. It was a new fighting force with new tactics, that used helicopters to provide aerial artillery and troop mobility. But the roots of these tactics lay in inter-departmental disputes between the army and air force in the years just after World War Two, as well as more general experience of the glider and airborne techniques that had been developed during the war.

After World War Two army strategists came to the conclusion that the use of gliders and parachutes for the mobile relocation of troops was both highly dangerous and inefficient. They also came to the conclusion that the US Air Force was too obsessed with the state-of-the-art technology of guided missiles, jets and rockets to pay much attention to the more humble logistics of troop transport. The army were the grunts, with their noses to the ground, and the ones who would pay the price of a ground war. They had to look out for themselves.

In the late 1940s the army and manufacturers of helicopters both studied the nascent helicopter operations employed by the British in Malaysia. There was a confluence of interest between them to exploit the new tactical possibilities that the helicopter seemed to present, both in providing fire during the critical approach phase of a combat assault and in its use as an aerial ambulance. However, their efforts were not co-ordinated in any meaningful way.

In the early 1950s officers watched bubble-glass H-13 helicopters – observation aircraft transformed into air ambulances for the Korean War – manoeuvre above hilly and difficult terrain with speed and agility. It took just a short leap of the imagination to see the potential they had for massive troop movements. Officers could also see how mountainous terrain like that of Korea favoured the defenders; the helicopter could help them to literally overleap this problem.

Starting in 1951 helicopter design had taken an evolutionary step forward as the older reciprocal engines were superseded by new gas-turbine ones. And in February 1954 the US Army proposed an industry-wide competition to research and develop a turbine-powered utility helicopter that could carry an 800 pound (363 kilogram) payload on a 200 nautical mile (227 mile/365 kilometre) round trip with a 100 knot (114 miles/183 kilometre an hour) cruising speed. Conceived as an aerial ambulance, it had to be constructed to permit field maintenance and to be transportable in a cargo plane. Twelve months later, in February 1955, the army announced that Bell's proposal, the XH-40, was the winner out of 20 entries and in June the company was awarded the contract to build three prototypes.

By October 1956 Bell had a test XH-40 up and flying. The military immediately ordered six of the helicopters for tests – which were rapidly followed by an order for production models. The army designated the helicopter the UH-1, which stood for 'helicopter, utility'; with grunt common sense and an ear for the practical, soldiers preferred to call it the 'Huey'. The name remained, even through later design modifications.

Although there were ambitious plans for the expanded use of the helicopter in battle, the original Huey was still thought of primarily as a mobile ambulance. This was reflected in the design of the craft itself. Its mid-section was made to fit a stretcher in lengthways and it was, comparatively, a very wide craft with room for the pilot and co-pilot to sit next to each other. Later developments, after the Huey's combat attributes had been recognized, thinned down the design to make it a leaner and more agile craft. The Bell Helicopter Model 204, an early prototype, was the basic design for the Huey and the later UH-1H (1962) and UH-1D (1963) were Model 205s. The 204's maximum cruising speed was 176 miles (283 kilometres) an hour and the flight, or mission, radius was 248 miles (400 kilometres).

Before the Huey, piston engines had been used to power US Army helicopters. However, the development of the 'turbo-shaft' engine, a technological offshoot of the turbo-jet, offered a new path forward. This powerful engine works by sucking in air and using the exhaust gases to drive a turbine which, in turn, provides power for the shaft. The output shaft drives the helicopter rotor through a transmission. The turbo-shaft engine was less complex than a piston engine; it also weighed less. The Huey started more easily than its predecessors and did not need to be warmed up before flight. The controls were so light that pilots who were new

to the aircraft often worked the pedals too hard, making the tail wag madly back and forth; a rookie pilot was easily identified by this characteristic 'Huey shuffle'.

Although the UH-1A came into service in June 1959 inter-departmental rivalry meant that its implementation and the development of later models was slow going. The air force took a dim view of the army's involvement in what they saw as their domain: the air.

In 1954 Lieutenant-General James M. Gavin, the director of army doctrine and combat development, had published an article called 'Cavalry ... and I Don't Mean Horses' in *Harper's* magazine. His theme was the mobility of troops in a nuclear war which, he argued, would incapacitate movement on the battlefield just when quick and agile transport of soldiers was exactly what was needed to exploit the devastating advantage of a nuclear explosion. His premise was that helicopters, the technological equivalents of cavalry horses on the battlefields of old, would fill that breach. Fast, powerful and efficient, they could deliver troops when and where necessary.

Five years later, Gavin led experiments with armed helicopters. Across-the-board co-ordination was lacking but on 15 January 1960 the army chief of staff

A Huey at Chu Pong mountain. Pilots risked their lives flying into enemy fire. As they neared the landing zone the helicopter was a prime target and many of them were heavily pitted with machine-gun fire. One heroic pilot flew his Huey non-stop from 6 a.m. to 10 p.m., ferrying in new troops and airlifting out the wounded.

established the Army Aircraft Requirements Review Board. Chaired by Lieutenant-General Gordon Rogers of the continental army command and afterwards known as the Rogers board, its brief was to evaluate the army aircraft development plan and review design concepts and industry proposals.

The Rogers board made two important recommendations: a design competition, this time for an observation aircraft; and an in-depth study to examine the concept of an air-fighting unit. Although its conclusions were overshadowed by the introduction of the concept of flexible response and events in Southeast Asia, the stage had been set for the use of the helicopter in a combat role.

THE VERDICT

IN CONVENTIONAL MILITARY terms, the battle of Ia Drang was a success. It was the first significant use of Huey helicopters, both to move troops adeptly to designated landing zones and in terms of the firepower unleashed by guns and rocket fire. The US airmobile division defeated three North Vietnamese regiments and prevented the communists sweeping down from the Highlands and cutting the country in two. It was a shining example of the effectiveness of dropping large units into action by helicopter.

Although more than three hundred Americans died in the battle the NVA lost nearly 2000 men. As the journalist and writer Stanley Karnow has pointed out, these figures are significant: they prompted General Westmoreland to argue that 'search and destroy' missions would gradually drain the enemy of strength and help the United States to win the war. By 'bleeding' the Vietnamese dry of men he would convince their commanders that they were on a foolhardy path that would significantly damage their culture and population for years to come. This realization would force them to sue for peace.

But Westmoreland's logic was doomed from the start. The American forces had decisively won the battle of Ia Drang but a 'total war' philosophy based on the lessons of this specific battle would eventually lose them the war.

The lessons of Vietnam were often inverted; it was a looking-glass war. What was unquestionably decisive in the short term – striking the NVA from a long distance through helicopter drops as it was massing for a major attack – was costly in the long term. Westmoreland miscalculated on two important points. First, he projected American values on to the Vietnamese who were waging a very different war. General Vo Nguyen Giap said later, 'We were not strong enough to drive half a million American troops out of Vietnam, but that wasn't our aim. We sought to break the will of the American government to continue the conflict. Westmoreland was wrong to count on his superior firepower to grind us down.' As Ho Chi Minh had said, prophetically, to the French in 1946: 'You can kill ten of my men for every one that I kill of yours. But even at those odds, you will lose and I will win.'

The second count on which Westmoreland was wrong was the effect of attrition on the public in the United States. They simply refused to accept Westmoreland's later kill-ratio of one American dead to every 2.6 Vietnamese. One dead American was one too many.

McNamara, who had been an ardent supporter of airmobility, was shaken by Westmoreland's request for an additional 41 500 troops the week after Ia Drang. On 30 November 1965, after a trip to Saigon, he wrote a memo to President Johnson. In contrast to his optimism earlier that summer, he was worried that the numbers were too much to bear and suggested that the administration should try to negotiate a peace settlement.

But the attraction of 'search and destroy' and Westmoreland's approach to the war was overwhelming; it had an unstoppable, institutional momentum. Even when the president was confronted by statistical projections, based on the battle of Ia Drang, of the foolishness of such a policy he would not accept their implications. Although the projections came from a general in the US marines rather than an anti-war think-tank, Johnson refused to face up to the fact that Westmoreland's war of attrition was, in actuality, the enemy's game.

Harold Moore, the battalion commander at the battle of Ia Drang, came to this conclusion in 1966. He believed that the NVA hit the air cavalry hard because it was intent on learning how to fight the American forces. The North Vietnamese had lost many men in the process but they had learned the ins and outs of this new type of war that was determined by the helicopter. Not only that – the North Vietnamese were later able to apply these lessons until they forced the Americans to fight their way. They were, in Sheehan's phrase, leading the army and the marine corps by the nose.

If Westmoreland's strategy was to work he had to take the offensive. But he was failing to do this: the Vietnamese had learned to initiate attacks and did so about 88 per cent of the time. They controlled the extent of American losses, raising and dropping the rate of attrition of the US army simply through their willingness to sacrifice their own people.

The Huey had proved decisive at Ia Drang. The irony is that its very effectiveness led the commanders of the American military to base a faulty strategy upon its use. As a result, the weapon and the war were a perfect fit: in Vietnam what seemed up was always down – and vice versa.

The Huey was never designed to carry heavy fighting equipment. Note the machine-gun mount bolted onto the hull. The Huey was quickly adapted to its fighting functions by retro-fitting guns and rockets onto its frame. Some machine-guns were even suspended from bungy cords from the top of the cabin. In war, improvisation can be crucial.

CHAPTER 6

THE
HARRIER

*The Airframe will not amount to a damn
until they get a machine that will act like
a humming-bird; go straight up, go
forward, come straight down and alight
like a humming-bird. It isn't easy but
somebody's going to do it.*

THOMAS EDISON (1847–1931)

*Without the Harrier there
could have been no Task Force.*

ADMIRAL SIR HENRY LEACH,
FIRST SEA LORD AND CHIEF OF NAVAL STAFF

THE CHALLENGE

THE FALKLANDS CONFLICT was one of the few wars in recent history that really was 'over by Christmas'. In the 10 weeks between 4 April and 14 June 1982 it achieved its objectives without spiralling out of control or degenerating into an unwinnable stalemate. From a military point of view it remains a classic example of political gain through conflict, the coming together of every wing of the armed forces in an operation with one overriding and specific goal: the expulsion of the Argentines from the Falkland Islands, and the return of the islands to British sovereignty. It was a political gamble intransigently taken by Margaret Thatcher. The British Royal Navy Task Force had at least one thing going for it: the total and committed backing of the prime minister who had ordered it into being.

At one stage this looked like being its only advantage. There was no other reason for optimism. The islands lay 10 000 miles (16 100 kilometres) away from the British mainland, but 400 miles (645 kilometres) from Argentina. The Task Force had to be assembled at breakneck speed, from scratch, and dispatched to an alien and utterly unforgiving theatre: the gale-lashed, sub-zero South Atlantic. Nor would this be some kind of nineteenth-century gunboat diplomacy. It would take more than a Union Jack unfurled in anger in San Carlos Bay on East Falkland Island to oust the invaders. They had not taken the Falklands/Malvinas on a whim. The dispute with Britain about Argentina's sovereignty over the islands cut deep into the Argentine national psyche and had been lodged high in the country's political agenda for decades. Much of the posturing was later seen for what it was – the shoring up of a regime looking to bolster its popularity with a display of nationalist derring-do – but in April 1982, as the Task Force set sail, this was all painfully in the future. The soldiers, sailors and airmen on their way south were under no illusions. If the peace talks mediated by the United States secretary of state, Alexander Haig, faltered a very real and determined enemy awaited them, one who was well armed, well resourced and highly motivated to win. However, the Task Force had a more pressing and immediate problem. What was it going to fight this war with?

Ten thousand miles (16 100 kilometres) presents no real problem for ships and the British could therefore expect to deliver a powerful naval and land force.

PREVIOUS SPREAD: The Harrier Jump Jet is not just a technological novelty to impress the crowds at air-shows. Armed with the most up-to-date ordnance, whether as here for ground attack, or for aerial dogfighting, it punches way above its weight.

This is where it all started, the so-called 'Flying Bedstead', just one of many outlandish-looking contraptions designed to take off and land vertically. The Americans, French, and Russians all experimented, but it was the Harrier, originally called the PS1127, which made it from drawing board to full operation.

Modern warfare is, however, determined from the air, and here they had a real problem. With no conventional aircraft-carriers any longer in service, and thousands of miles away from the nearest friendly air base, sailors and soldiers would be fighting alone without the Tornadoes and Phantoms of the Royal Air Force (RAF), completely at the mercy of the Argentine fighters and bombers that would sweep in over the sea from bases barely an hour away from the disputed islands. The only solution to the problem lay with a 20-year-old oddity that had never yet fired a shot in anger: the Harrier or Sea-Harrier as the Navy version was called. But there was room to take only 20 of these aircraft.

A huge responsibility rested on this handful of jets, huddled together on the decks and in the hangars of the helicopter cruisers HMS *Hermes* and HMS *Invincible*. It was nothing less than to provide air cover for the whole fleet and, later, for the invading forces over thousands of square miles of ocean – and to spearhead the assault on enemy positions, almost certainly well defended, and in particular on the Argentines' only Falklands airstrip, at Port Stanley. Their pilots were expected to engage in dogfights with supersonic fighters, attack ground targets defended by guided missiles and mount patrols searching for Exocet-bearing Argentine bombers and Argentine naval vessels – round the clock, and from two tiny flight decks, in the worst weather conditions imaginable. They had barely weeks of ocean transit in which to prepare for the toughest challenge of their professional military careers.

Everyone knew that the Sea-Harrier was, at best, an ingenious compromise. It could take off and land vertically, hovering like a helicopter, but precious little else. It was too slow and too old to hold its own against front-line interceptors like the Mirages and Daggers flown by the Argentines. The Royal Navy was forced to use Sea-Harriers because, without full-size aircraft-carriers, they were the only combat jets that could cope with the much smaller ships that had been converted to aircraft duties. Nobody would have chosen to go to war with only these aircraft, and with so few of them.

For 20 years the manufacturers of the Harrier had been insisting that it had enormous potential and that its ability to land and take off vertically was only one of its assets. Few air forces other than the RAF had believed them. The US marines liked it because they needed to be able to dispense with formal runways. India and Spain had also bought some. Nobody else had. The Soviets had their own version of a jump jet, the Yak-36 *Forger*, but it was widely thought to be even less interesting than the British plane. The Harrier had been admired at air shows, and

A Royal Navy Sea-Harrier hovering about to make a vertical landing. With Britain no longer able to afford full-size aircraft-carriers it was this unique ability that allowed the Navy to carry on using jet combat aircraft on ships with decks too short for conventional naval jets.

applauded for its technical innovations, but had somehow failed to become credible. All that was about to change.

The next few months would provide the sternest test imaginable for the Sea-Harrier. The aircraft would come of age, or die an ignominious death, its critics proved right. The Harrier was too slow, too 'clever' to be of any real use in real combat, they would say. Luckily for the British, the men who flew the jump jet were not among the scoffers. They knew that it could do more than just hover pointlessly in the air. They also knew that their lives, and those of thousands of British soldiers and sailors, depended on their being right. As the Task Force set sail on 4 April, the 20 Sea-Harriers faced their toughest challenge: not only to take on a conventional air force, but do so against years of under-investment and lack of technological upgrading. Would the aircraft prove to be incapable of carrying enough of the right kind of weapons far and fast enough to have any effect? And would its inability to fly supersonic prove suicidal? These questions were not academic. If the Sea-Harrier failed, then so would the Task Force.

THE BATTLE

THE SIGNS WERE NOT auspicious; the Harrier had been in service for nearly 13 years by 1982 and had never been tested in combat. Most observers remained impressed but sceptical, happy to see it maintaining its role as a technological flag-waver. This would not necessarily have mattered had the British invested in adequate armaments and avionics for the jet, but they had not. Its navigational system was obsolete, it had no capacity for releasing chaff (bundles of aluminium-coated plastic used to fool the radar of incoming missiles), no dedicated air-to-air missile to prevent it being a sitting duck in hostile skies; and it had not been cleared to use laser-guided weapons or anti-radar missiles – all by now standard air-warfare equipment. Its ordnance was limited to 68mm rockets and 1000 pound (450 kilogram) bombs. Even more ludicrously, although it was intended that the Harrier should operate from ships, no one had thought fit to adapt its inertial navigation systems to function on a moving deck. All of this would have to be put right on the long voyage to the South Atlantic, and later. It would be a staggering achievement even without taking into account what the Harrier was expected to do in the air.

The forces ranged against the Task Force were formidable. The Fuerza Aerea Argentina (FAA) and the Comando de Aviacion Naval Argentina (CANA) could put up 200 aircraft, most of which outclassed the Harrier in terms of orthodox air-to-air combat. Many of these were front-line Mach 2 Dassault-Breuget Mirage delta-wing fighters. The Israelis used a version of this plane, and had shown in two wars against the Arab nations just how effective a weapon it could be. And it was not only numbers that made British observers pessimistic. The Sea-Harrier was not designed to take on formations of fast-attack jets; it was at its best against large, subsonic single intruders approaching from predictable directions. To take on a Mirage, attacking from a low or high altitude, at speeds hundreds of miles an hour faster than the Harrier could fly was going to be a tall order.

In addition the Argentines had bombers: American Sky Hawks that had seen service in Vietnam; home-built short-range Pucaras that would pose a real threat to any amphibious landings; long-range British Canberras; and, perhaps most crucially, 10 Super Etendards; not in themselves particularly dangerous, but each of them carried the French-built Exocet air-to-surface guided missile capable – as proved to be the case – of destroying whole ships. The Falklands Argentine garrison could be reinforced and supplied by eight Hercules transport planes, as well as a host of helicopters and smaller supply planes. In-air refuelling capacity came in the shape of two Lockheed KC-103 tankers, which would drastically improve the range of the missile-carrying Super Etendards and bomb-laden Sky Hawks – although not that of the Mirages, which were not equipped to take advantage of the system. The Argentines also had the aged but still operational aircraft-carrier, the *Veinticinco de Mayo* (although this relied on the *General Belgrano* for protection) as well as the airstrip at Port Stanley.

Argentina's principal strike weapon would remain the French-built Mirage, and the Sea-Harrier pilots concentrated on this adversary. The Mirage III had a radius of action of about 500 nautical miles (926 kilometres), a proportion of which was flown at low level for penetration and escape. The Argentines had a squadron of about 17 of these aircraft and, in addition, at least 42 Israeli-built Daggers (strike fighters with a visual air-combat capability) which were equivalent to the Mirage V. It was later discovered that Peru had made ten of its force of Mirages available to Argentina, giving its air chief Lami Dozo a total of 70 Mirages and Daggers. The prospect of only 20 subsonic Sea-Harriers taking off into the South Atlantic fog from heaving, pitching decks, and having to find their way back – often in zero visibility at the very furthest reaches of their fuel range – cannot have caused him too many sleepless nights, in the beginning at least.

In the event, much of the AAF threat was minimized because the British succeeded in forcing it to use Argentine home air bases so reducing its combat time over the Falklands. And with the sinking of the *Belgrano*, the aircraft-carrier it protected was effectively removed from the war. Rear-Admiral John 'Sandy' Woodward did what he could do to increase the odds by placing his own aircraft-carrier group as far away from the Argentine air bases and as close to the Falklands as possible. That meant that only the British could, in theory, keep planes in the air

Two RAF Harriers practising their ground attack skills. At low altitudes its subsonic top speed is no disadvantage. With its manoeuvrability, and ability to operate from any kind of landing strip, even clearings in the woods, it has remained one of NATO's principal strike weapons.

over the islands at any time. Since the Battle of Britain this has been an invaluable strategic advantage for an air force suffering considerable numerical inferiority and, as with the Battle of Britain, it was to prove crucial.

Questions of equipment and weaponry are academic without taking into account the men who will use them, their training, morale and ability to operate under pressure. Here, perhaps, the British were not as ill-prepared as it might at first have looked. The men who flew the Sea-Harriers had two things in their favour. First, as part of NATO, all British pilots were accustomed to performing at the very highest levels in exercises conducted all over the world in many different theatres, in collaboration with other air forces. And because most of their battle preparation was conceived with the mighty Soviet Air Force in mind, they were accustomed to pitting themselves against overwhelming odds. Second, their training was less inappropriate than that of most other members of the Task Force, many of whom were having to learn what war in the South Atlantic would mean for the first time. It was not just that the pilots were used to exercises in the north of Scotland, although this would be enormously helpful. It was that at least one of the two squadrons sailing south was led by a man who had for years successfully campaigned for air-combat training for his pilots. Squadron Leader Nigel 'Sharkey' Ward, commanding officer of 801 Squadron, had beaten into his men the need to learn the art of dogfighting against the best the world's air forces could throw at them.

The Sea-Harrier may have been designed to oppose slow-moving maritime reconnaissance planes, but Ward neverthless ensured that his pilots received rigorous combat practice against supersonic fighters. It paid off. Only a short while before the Falklands conflict began, his squadron had achieved impressive results in an exercise in Norway against American Aggressor squadrons, élite formations of F5s and F16s that had been formed to provide Allied air forces with the toughest air-combat simulation in the world. These pretend-enemies had been repeatedly amazed by the success achieved by the Sea-Harriers, planes they had every right to believe were far inferior in performance to their supersonic, state-of-the-art jet interceptors.

The Sea-Harrier pilots knew that the aircraft was more than just a plane capable of taking off and landing vertically: it was a weapons system that in skilled and confident hands could take on, and beat, anything that any air force in the world could throw against it. This knowledge went some way toward calming their nerves as they sailed to face a force ten times their number, and in many ways made them more sanguine than the Argentines expected.

This level of confidence was not shared by their British superiors. The Admiralty was pessimistic. Its experts doubted that this tiny handful of planes could survive for long and predicted an attrition rate of one Harrier a day. Had they been proved right – and there were some who thought that even this was being generous – air cover would have been lost within three weeks. Luckily they were wrong – although losses did reach this level for three worrying days in succession in early May, reminding everybody that their initial gloom had not been a case of crying wolf.

As the Task Force sailed south it became increasingly clear that the Sea-Harriers would be used on both defensive and offensive missions, keeping Argentine jets at bay and also attacking the Port Stanley runway. This was to be a vital target. Although it was short it was feared that, with its portable arrester equipment similar to that used on aircraft-carriers, it would be able to support Mirages as well as the slower, but still deadly, A4 Sky Hawks and Pucaras that would spearhead AAF attacks on British ships. This fear proved groundless, to the Task Force's considerable relief, but it was nevertheless vital that the British cripple the runway and the threat of continuous short-range attacks that it posed.

The voyage to the Falklands gave the squadrons – 800 based aboard HMS *Hermes* the flagship and the larger of the two, and 801 on HMS *Invincible* – the chance to gain battle readiness, with equipment and, more important, in tactics. The key element in their strategy was a flying formation called the 'hook' or 'Polish heart'. British Harriers flew in pairs, each pilot long familiar with the other. Orthodox flying tactics dictated that a combat pair comprised a lead plane and a wingman who was there only to protect his partner, but the navy had developed a looser strategy that gave equal status and considerable autonomy to each plane. This required perfect precision and co-ordination if it was to work. Essentially, the 'Polish heart' was a kind of aerial pincer movement in which the pilot and wingman attacked head-on and then split left and right before weaving behind the oncoming aircraft and working round the back into prime firing position. It was to prove highly effective every time it was used against the Mirages and Daggers.

The navy and RAF exchange pilots who made up the two squadrons practised all the skills they were going to need. Taking off and landing in pitch darkness, with cockpit illumination kept to a minimum, took nerve even in an experienced pilot. Preparations for combat soon became as close to routine as they ever could: endless variations of the vault from the 'ski jump' into the inky cold black of the Atlantic night, 'transitioning' from semi-vertical flight to fully horizontal wingborne flight as quickly as possible, putting the nozzles aft, raising the flap and undercarriage, getting radar on line and preparing weapons, before taking up position at 1000 feet (305 metres) at 400 knots. Gunnery and missile exercises sharpened and honed the reflexes that keep a fighter pilot alive. Here too, the squadron commanders pronounced themselves satisfied. Initial results were encouraging and morale was high.

By the end of April the Task Force was in a combat zone. The next contact they would have would be with an enemy. And sure enough, on 21 April a high-level, subsonic, radar contact belonging to a high-flying Argentine Boeing 707 reconnaissance plane, that was spotted a few times but always avoided engagement,

was monitored. From that moment on, two significant changes were introduced. It would be standard operational practice to have a Sea-Harrier either airborne or in full readiness on deck round the clock. And the Task Force declared a Missile Exclusion Zone which had to be guarded zealously. By now it had moved to a full wartime footing and abandoned many of the routines of peacetime. Harriers were kept fully armed, even when parked in the hangar. On deck they would ordinarily have been pointed out to sea in case there was accidental gunfire but space was now limited and sailors had to skirt their way round jets carrying live ammunition that were pointing not out to sea, but at them.

There was even a new paint job, as each Sea-Harrier was given its Atlantic camouflage of dark charcoal grey. Engines were uprated to war levels. Worries grew about the proximity of Exocet attack as the force neared the Falklands. The Harriers' first operation was to support Vulcan bomber (V-bomber) runs against the Port Stanley airstrip. These missions were hugely costly in fuel – the bombers flew 6000 miles (9655 kilometres) from the Ascension Islands and were refuelled continuously on both legs of the journey by a fleet of 10 air tankers – and results were marginal. Ward has written that he and his pilots were adamant that they

Developed by a Navy officer doing a thesis at Southampton University, the 'ski jump' was a brilliant innovation. It allowed the Sea-Harrier to take off safely and effectively from its shortened deck runways using a fraction of the fuel needed for vertical take-offs.

could do the job of disabling the runway better themselves.

There would be two phases to their involvement in the conflict: before the land assault and after it when they would protect the landing forces. Phase one would be crucial and would pitch the Harriers against the AAF Mirages. The priority was to ensure that the fast-jets would have to fly from their home bases in Argentina and be unable to use the Port Stanley airstrip. Although the mainland was less than an hour away, the 400 mile (645 kilometre) distance was enough to make fuel a problem for the Mirages, and would reduce combat time over the islands to about 25 minutes for each jet. The Mirages would also be forced to use their dwindling stock of external fuel tanks, which would have to be jettisoned. It was difficult for the Argentines to replace the tanks so numbers of Mirages would in effect be grounded because they were unable to increase their range.

The attacks on the runway would therefore take on a new form. To supplement the V-bombers, still plugging away to very little effect, the Harriers would bomb the airstrip as a routine operation on their way to Combat Air Patrol (CAP) positions. But these plans were a diversion from the real challenge. What would happen when the Harriers really started to mix it with the Mirages? Was their early optimism pie in the sky?

The first encounters with the Mirages were cautious affairs. The Argentines had installed good area-surveillance radar on the islands which kept the Mirages informed of all CAP movements. The first few contacts were inconclusive. The Argentine jets shadow-boxed with the British aircraft, drawing the Harriers to them before making away at speed. The Mirages attacked from high level, firing their missiles from maximum, and often beyond maximum, range (due as much to bad tactical advice from the ground as to pilot timidity). This was cat and mouse; both sides concentrated on increasing their feel for the enemy and gathering information and expertise. The Mirages were keeping their distance – but for how long?

Guns were first fired in anger by a Harrier pilot surprised to see a T-34 Pucara fly across his gun sight, but with no result. There were more encounters with Mirages but they too took the by now familiar form of a long-range discharge of missiles followed by a rapid retreat to the Argentine mainland. Finally, HMS *Glamorgan* tracked the arrival of two Mirages flying low and hard and showing no signs of turning back. They were committed to a fight – one that was to prove the first of a number of decisive encounters. The fast-jets were 25 miles (40 kilometres) out; then 20 miles (32 kilometres) and closing at a mile every few seconds. Steve Thomas and Paul Barton of 801 Squadron now had their chance to

The Royal Navy had to squeeze twenty Sea-Harriers onto its two ships, HMS Invincible, *and HMS* Hermes, *transporting them 10 000 miles to face the Argentines, who had over ten times this number of planes. The pilots knew that the Task Force relied on them for protection from air attack while at sea, and after mounting their land assault.*

prove the worth of the Harrier and the 'Polish heart' tactic so central to 'Sharkey' Ward's combat plans.

Barton split to the left and built up lateral separation from the two Mirages so that he could turn back in on them without flying through their formation. He accelerated and steadied. Eleven miles (18 kilometres). This was the Mirages' last chance to turn back; the battle was joined. The four jets were now converging at one mile (1.5 kilometres) every 3 seconds. Thomas activated his radar beam and gained visual contact at 4 miles (6.5 kilometres). He was unable to lock on and then, to his horror, saw two shapes detaching themselves from the Mirages. Missiles. He whistled past and wrenched his stick back to pull the Harrier round and give chase. There was, in fact, no cause for alarm; the 'shapes' later proved to be fuel tanks being jettisoned. And, in any case, the Mirages were in poor formation, vulnerable to the second Harrier approaching from the right. The 'Polish heart' snapped shut; Steve Thomas got a missile off – 'Fox Two away' ... 'Splash One Mirage'. The second Mirage was last seen diving vainly for the clouds with a Sidewinder air-to-air missile in deadly pursuit. They later learned that the Mirage had been damaged in the encounter, and then destroyed by trigger-happy Argentine ground forces on the Falklands as it dropped through the cloud base, trailing smoke and flames.

In the next encounter with the Argentines the Sea-Harriers pursued two low-flying Argentine Canberra fighter-bombers; they too were hunted down and 'splashed'. The British tally was now two Mirages and two Canberras without loss. The British Sea-Harrier had seized the initiative and the Argentines were in prime position to rethink their attitude to it; overnight it had ceased to be an aircraft with an uncertain reputation, and instead become the *'Muertas Negras'*, or Black Death.

These early successes did nothing to diminish the punishing routine of endless 24-hour patrols and full combat alerts. The Sea-Harriers were also pressing home their attacks on the airstrip which was still operating despite further V-Bomber raids. The action switched to the sea when a single Sea-Harrier flying north-east from the Task Force used its Blue Fox air-interceptor radar to verify that an Argentine naval force had split in two as the prelude to a major pincer attack on the British fleet. At the heart of the formation were the Argentine aircraft-carrier and the *General Belgrano*. The *Belgrano* was sunk on the following day, 2 May. This destroyed any chance of peace talks forestalling conflict – and once again provided evidence of the value of the Sea-Harrier's on-board radar, which was still regarded with scepticism by the Admiralty.

Twenty fighters cannot be everywhere they are needed even when they are flying to the limit of their operational capacity. And on 4 May the extent to which the combat air patrol cordon was stretched became clear. A group of patrolling Sea-Harriers was pulled off station to pursue radar contacts picked up by the ships and, fatally, left a hole in the cordon. It was all the Argentines needed – a chink in the air cover at last – and they flew in two of their Exocet-carrying Super Etendards. One missile launch later, HMS *Sheffield* was in flames. Another blow to the Task Force soon followed. A Sea-Harrier flown by Lieutenant Nick Taylor was shot down by radar-directed 30mm anti-aircraft fire in a low-level attack – the aircraft's first Falklands fatality. Other pilots questioned the timing of the attack which had taken place just after the latest V-Bomber run against the airstrip when the AAF were still on full alert.

Despite the initial trepidation that the Sea-Harriers would be stretched to the limit by the superior Mirages, not a single plane was lost to aerial combat. Much more dangerous was ground fire – and the weather. The largest single loss in one action occurred when two Sea-Harriers flown by experienced officers disappeared at sea. There was only one plausible explanation. Two exhausted pilots must have collided in the South Atlantic gales and mist.

This left 801 Squadron down to six jets and nine pilots and in desperate need of reinforcements. The only problem was that no Sea-Harriers were available – and it would take three years to build more. The only ones under construction were destined for the Indian navy, and there was no question of them being commandeered. There was one answer: land-based RAF GR3 Harriers would have to be taken from operational service in Germany, converted to take off and land at sea while *en route* to the South Atlantic – and be flown by pilots who had never flown from a ship-deck. Getting the aircraft to their destination was an epic in itself. Some arrived via the ill-fated *Atlantic Conveyor* which was later destroyed by an Exocet missile. Otherwise it was a marathon 9 hour journey via the Ascension Islands, being refuelled time and time again in the air. Once on station, the RAF Harriers had to be modified for action over the water, although they would principally be used in their original ground-attack role to support the land assault.

The Sea-Harriers and RAF Harriers saw action without a break right up to the cessation of hostilities. They did all that was expected of them, and more. They inflicted large levels of losses on the Argentines, destroying every class of plane sent up against them. Most significantly, however, they proved more than a match for the Mirage. The truth was that the Mirage was simply outclassed by the Harrier, and the Argentines knew it. The Sea-Harriers operated at every altitude and in every role. They protected the landings by duelling with the Pucaras and Sky Hawks at under 250 feet (75 metres) and chased off reconnaissance aircraft at 40 000 feet (12 200 metres). Canberras, Mirages, Pucaras, Sky Hawks and even a Lockheed Hercules transport plane fell victim to the Sea-Harrier. No other aircraft could have done what it did. The plane's combination of short, ski-jump-assisted take-off and vertical landing made it possible for it to fly in even the worst weather. On numerous occasions a Sea-Harrier, running low on fuel and shrouded in rain and mist, would inch its way back to the radar signal that designated the *Hermes* or *Invincible*, and lower itself gingerly through the swirling cloud, guided down by spotlights to execute a perfect landing on a pitching deck. And once in the air it proved itself anything but compromised in performance. Its adaptability meant that 20 aircraft did the work of twice that number. Its ability to punch way above its weight ensured it a decisive role in what was, until its final stages, a desperately balanced conflict. Admiral Sir Henry Leach had been right: without it there would have been no Task Force.

THE MACHINE

THE STORY OF THE HARRIER is a classic tale of British innovation and compromise. Like the hovercraft and Concorde, it was the product of post-war 'white-heat' technology, a brilliant marriage of design daring and the confidence of a country that still saw itself as a global superpower – but its development was marred at every step by indecision and faltering timidity in the face of shrinking budgets and confusion over what exactly Britain's defence requirements were. The aircraft is still a show-stopper, even 30 years after it first achieved vertical take-off – a fully armed combat jet roaring to a halt, hovering above the tarmac and landing dextrously on its undercarriage of two outriggers under the wing tips and the distinctive in-line wheels front and back. For much of its early operational life this was all it was credited with being able to achieve. That changed in the early months of 1982.

The Harrier was the product of a quest as old as powered flight: the search for vertical take-off and landing. An aircraft that can do this is freed from having to use a fixed runway or airfield. It can be deployed in a far wider variety of locations than would otherwise be the case, and be kept away from air bases, always prime targets for attack in war. Its drawback, in the era of the Mach 2 supersonic jet fighter, is compromised performance. It is not much use being able to stagger into the air if the aircraft, once aloft, is easy meat to a conventionally launched enemy. This had always been the case with the helicopter which had never been involved in orthodox dogfights. Instead it used its ability to hover and to rise and drop vertically as a reconnaissance aircraft or troop-carrier. Latterly, the helicopter has devised for itself a more offensive role, but as a gunship attack plane and not a fighter.

Anyone thinking about how to achieve powered lift has to think about how to achieve take-off. The key element in getting a heavier-than-air object aloft is lift, and this is produced by propelling an aerofoil, or wing, through the air. With enough speed, the pressure above the wing is sufficiently different from the pressure beneath for the effects of gravity to be overcome, and up the object goes.

Consequently, the orthodox aeroplane engine is designed to operate horizontally, along the body of the aircraft, pushing forward; it is the wings moving through the air at speed that produce the lift. Only a vertical rocket creates lift with thrust alone, rather than wing surface, but it is limited to going in only one direction: straight up or, if launched from an already airborne aircraft, straight along.

For the first 40 years of aviation history vertical take-off was science fiction, simply because there was no engine powerful enough to provide the required lift. Even helicopters have this problem, and achieve the fast forward velocity needed for the wings to be capable of counteracting gravity only by tilting their main rotor. This changed towards the end of World War Two with the advent of the jet engine, capable of producing far more thrust for its weight than any propeller piston engine. From this point on there were numerous fairly comical attempts to break free from the constraints of orthodox take-off and landing technology.

The early models took one of two basic forms. They were either 'tail-sitters' or 'flat-risers'. The tail-sitters were jet versions of the more familiar rocket. In other words, they took off while pointing straight up into the sky, held in position by rigs similar to those used at Cape Kennedy for space launches. The idea was simplicity itself: fire a jet engine straight down and use its thrust to propel the aircraft straight up. The flat-riser also adapted the strategy of having a vertically angled engine, but this time it was placed in the middle of the aircraft. It was like a very powerful hovercraft and had the advantage that the pilot, sitting on top of the engine, was already facing the right way. The best example of this was the so-called 'Flying Bedstead', or Thrust Measuring Rig, built by Rolls-Royce, which achieved vertical sustained take-offs as early as 1953. The 'tail-sitter' had the more difficult job of 'transitioning' from vertical to horizontal flight. This involved the nerve-racking business of levelling the rising craft and moving off in straight flight – and repeating the process, in reverse order, to land. The most advanced 'tail-sitter', the American X13 'Verti-Jet', demonstrated that in principle V(ertical) T(ake-off and) L(anding) (VTL)was possible – but impracticable in this primitive form.

Reconciling vertical take-off with level flight was proving insurmountable. Endless variations were tried: aircraft with five different engines, four pointing down, and one lengthways; aircraft with rotating jet engines on the wing tips; fat bumble-bee fuselages with cruciform wings and tails. They all looked as if they came straight out of a Gerry Anderson serial.

It was becoming clear that for any VTL aircraft to have a credible chance of reaching operational readiness it would have to be simple, robust, and ideally powered by a single engine. Rolls-Royce and Short Brothers in the United Kingdom, and Dessault in France, were all producing experimental composite engines to meet this need. Two main conditions applied. The crucial issue for an engine producing thrust in a variety of different directions, across different axes, was its relationship with the aircraft's centre of gravity. Any engine moving from horizontal to vertical would need to be right on the centre of gravity. If it was placed at the rear it would never be strong enough in the vertical to compensate for the huge imbalance. That ruled out the orthodox rear position. Nor should the engine's own centre of gravity be too far forward. An engine in the rear usually relied on the weight of the cockpit equipment to provide balance; placed nearer the front it would require compensating weight at the back – but the cockpit would not be there to provide it. It took years to solve this problem.

By the late 1950s four major powers were actively working on the problem: the British, the Americans, the French and the Soviets whose 'flat-riser' – the Yak-36 *Forger* – successfully achieved vertical take-off in 1958. But the British had one major advantage: the best engine, provided by Rolls-Royce. The intervention of a serious and committed aircraft manufacturer was now required to take the idea from drawing board to airfield, and the Hawker Siddeley Group did this, in close collaboration with Rolls-Royce. Hawker Siddeley was the company which, under the inspired leadership of its chief designer Sir Stanley Camm, had already produced a number of key British fighters, most famously the Hurricane, mainstay of the Battle of Britain and the aircraft credited with more German kills than all other British planes combined. It was producing the Hunter, a front-line jet fighter for the RAF, but was thrown into panic by a 1957 defence White Paper that at a stroke cancelled further development of what by now was its single product. Disaster loomed, and only diversification into other aviation defence projects saved the company. This was the background to its decision to focus on the VTL project as an alternative lifeline.

Hawker's designers and engineers turned to France to see the form this might take. What particularly caught their eye was the Gyropter proposal devised by the French designer Michel Wibault, who had first come up with the concept of a single engine capable of providing 90 degrees of variable thrust. His idea was to have a turboshaft driving four centrifugal compressors in the sides of the fuselage. All the pilot would have to do would be to swivel the nozzles by turning the casing surrounding each blower, like a hot-air hand-drier whose angle can be altered to dry the face. Gone was the need for up to five separate engines. Camm had fortuitously come across the Gyropter at the Paris Air Show in June 1957. He joined forces with Stanley Hooker, an engine designer, and set to work on what was to be called the P1127.

The wing of this new prototype was mounted high in order to keep it clear of the engines. The unusual undercarriage layout was forced on its designers to facilitate vertical landings and keep the wheels out of the way. Another technical problem concerned stability at low speeds. The wings would provide no lift when the plane was in a hover and using the joy stick would therefore be useless for controlling the aircraft's pitch (movement in the vertical) and yaw (movement in the horizontal). The answer was to equip it with four compressed air 'puffers', one at each corner. The pilot would use these to keep the jet level and stable. The cockpit, however, was kept as simple as possible, the only difference to the Gyropter being the addition of a nozzle control next to the throttle. After air-bed and wind-tunnel testing in Britain and America, the first P1127 prototype was ready for its maiden trial. And on 21 October 1960 Bill Bedford, Hawker's chief test pilot, achieved the first hesitant hover with the plane tethered to the ground for safety. The power was provided by the first version of what to this day is the Harrier's primary engine, the Rolls-Royce Pegasus, providing 11 000 pounds (4990 kilograms) of thrust.

After a month of becoming accustomed to the tricks required to master vertical take-off, the tethers were released and Bedford was free to push the PS1127 forward, taxiing slowly a few feet off the ground. The original prototype was supplemented by a second one with a more powerful engine designed to test the new aircraft's performance in standard flight. The Hawker test pilots now set out to crack the art of 'transitioning'. Despite the odd heavy landing, it was clear that the prototype more than fulfilled its early promise. Capable of landing on grass, and robust enough for up to 3000 hours of continuous service, it was ideal for the flexible combat role already envisaged for it. Now all Hawker and Rolls-Royce had to do was sell the aircraft.

The Royal Navy and the RAF were both sceptical. In 1963 Bedford landed a Kestrel, as the jump jet was first called, on the aircraft-carrier *Ark Royal*. However, the navy was not keen to invest in the production of a jet combat aircraft that was unable to fly supersonically. There was also a political problem. The capacity to take off and land vertically would remove the need for a runway. But the navy was still committed to keeping its large aircraft-carriers, huge and expensive though they were, and a VTL aircraft would make them obsolete. The RAF, too, were unconvinced that with only 13 500 pounds (8600 kilograms) of thrust, the aircraft could carry enough of a payload. It was time for the fledgling to be properly evaluated. In 1962, a squadron of 10 pilots from Britain, the United States and Germany convened in Norfolk to do just that. The Kestrel had a more sophisticated wing and tail section than the PS1127, and 'puffers' capable of working up as well as down. It was clearly a world leader in operational VTL technology. After 900 sorties it was undeniable that this was an aircraft that was here to stay – if only the military powers would let it.

Hawker Siddeley was planning to develop a follow-up to the Kestrel. The P1154 would be called the Harrier, after another, larger, hovering bird of prey, and would be supersonic with a bigger engine and the capability of igniting fuel in the compressor nozzles to increase thrust. Again the British government pulled the carpet from under the company's feet and cancelled the Harrier along with the TSR2 and plans for a VTL transport plane. Hawker persevered with the Harrier, and compromised by keeping it subsonic. The result was half-way between the

THE HARRIER

RAF GR3 Harriers were sent to the South Atlantic to replace the Royal Navy Sea-Harriers lost in action. Not one Harrier, or Sea-Harrier, was ever lost in aerial combat, however.

At the time of the Falklands, the British had only one spare Sea-Harrier back in Britain. It would have taken three years to build further replacements – hence the decision to use RAF Harriers and convert them to use at sea.

Nicknamed 'La Muerta Negra' – meaning 'Black Death' – by the Argentines, the Harrier was greatly feared for its combat capabilities. The RAF and the Royal Navy pilots had trained for years against the best fighter jets in use by Allied Air Forces, honing their dogfighting skills, and building confidence. Argentine pilots, although extremely brave, simply did not have this level of preparation.

RAF camouflage – Sea-Harriers used grey

Sidewinder air-to-air missile

Cockpit

Radar

Air intake

Pegasus engine main fan

Directional nozzle

Rear jet nozzle, set here for vertical take-off – it would swivel to horizontal for level flight

4 x nozzles   External fuel tanks

The GR3 Harrier was used primarily as a ground attack aircraft. The Royal Navy Sea-Harriers, flying from HMS *Hermes* and HMS *Invincible*, did the bulk of the fighting

It was only because the Harrier could land and take off vertically that the British had any air cover at all. By 1981 the Royal Navy had got rid of its large aircraft carriers. The Hermes *and* Invincible *only had short runways, and only a jump-jet could use them.*

The Spanish, the Indians and the American Marines all use Harriers. The Soviets have their own version of a jump jet, the Yak 36. Next generation Harriers are being built by British Aerospace in conjunction with the American corporation, McDonnell Douglas. There are even plans to produce ones capable of supersonic flight.

Directional puffer   Outrigger undercarriage

After extensive training in the north of Scotland, the Harrier pilots found the terrain of the Falklands very similar

Kestrel and the P1154. The aircraft boasted a 19,000 pound (8600 kilogram) Pegasus engine, an altered wing design and a new internal navigation and weapons system with a head-up display. It was now ready for active service and the RAF was one of four armed forces to use it. The others were the US marines and the Spanish and Indian navies. The American version, the AV-8A, was put into service against huge political opposition in the United States, while the Spanish 'Matador' was put to sea on board the country's one aircraft-carrier.

By the mid-1960s it was obvious that, for all its attempts to forestall the inevitable, the Royal Navy was going to lose its four remaining big aircraft-carriers and with them the capacity to fly sea-borne fixed wing aircraft like the Sea Vixen, the Buccaneer or, most recently, the American F-4 Phantom. Once again Hawker Siddeley tried to interest the Admiralty in the Harrier, conducting VTL trials off a helicopter cruiser, HMS *Blake*. A problem emerged. Vertical take-off with a full load of weapons was very heavy on fuel. This reduced the Harrier's payload and its range when it was carrying the weapons. The navy needed a compromise aircraft capable of short take-off and of landing vertically when, with weapons and fuel expended, it would be much lighter.

Hawker Siddeley set out to produce a version of the Harrier specifically geared to operating at sea. By 1975 it had the answer called, not very surprisingly, the Sea-Harrier. It was a modified version of the RAF's GR1 Harrier (GR stands for ground attack and reconnaissance). Better all-round visibility was produced with a cockpit-seating arrangement 11 inches (28 centimetres) higher than that in the GR1; the aircraft was protected from the elements, particularly salt air and water, and it was fitted with the on-board Blue Fox air-interceptor radar system that was to prove so crucial in the Falklands. The navy had fixed-wing fighter capacity, but to make use of this it required a ship half-way between a full-blown aircraft-carrier and a helicopter cruiser – the Sea-Harrier did not need steam catapults and arrester gear but would require more than just the deck space available on helicopter ships. Essential to the navy's deployment of the aircraft was something much more banal than new engines or vectored thrust nozzles. The fruit of a Southampton University postgraduate thesis by Lieutenant-Commander Douglas Taylor, it was a ski jump – that distinctive, upward-curling lip at the end of the aircraft-carrier deck. This brilliantly simple innovation provided a multitude of unforeseen advantages over using a flat deck.

The Sea-Harrier could take off at half the speed required on a flat deck, using one-third less deck length and carrying up to 10 000 pounds (4540 kilograms) of weapons payload. The ski jump was also far safer for the pilot. The moment of take-off is always the most dangerous, and the last-minute vertical surge the ski jump provided would give a stricken pilot more time to eject in the event of engine failure. It was the latest in a long line of British aircraft-carrier technology developed by the navy which included the steam catapult and the angled deck.

With its range now extended to 400 miles (645 kilometres), and its ability to carry Sidewinder air-to-air missiles and cover 20 000 square miles (51 800 kilometres) of ocean with its reconnaissance radar systems, the Sea-Harrier was ready to take up its role as the navy's primary strike aircraft.

The RAF had meanwhile been developing the GR1 Harrier (soon replaced by the more advanced GR3), for its role in NATO where flexibility in the face of the then-major threat posed by Warsaw Pact land forces and the vulnerability of air bases to tactical nuclear strikes, was a major requirement. The camouflaged Harrier hidden in wooded clearings across the plains of north Germany became a familiar sight on NATO exercises. Once again, however, although the advantages of VTL were tangibly obvious, no other air force seemed persuaded of the Harrier's virtues, or inclined to consider producing alternative versions. Even the RAF, still concerned about its lack of supersonic speed, was accused of being half-hearted in its deployment of the aircraft.

THE VERDICT

DURING THE FALKLANDS CONFLICT the Sea-Harrier, by virtue of its unique take-off and landing capacity, operated where no conventional jet could have operated and went on to prove itself formidable in the air. Some of its pilots claimed it still did not receive the recognition it deserved, but in the popular imagination there can be little doubt that it became as much a part of the Falklands experience as yomping, the Exocet and the Paras. It abundantly proved itself everything its designers had hoped it would be.

It was the product of a unique moment in British military history, borne on a wave of post-war technological inventiveness, but suffering in an era of shrinking British technological confidence, and confusions about military priorities. British Aerospace continue to develop new models of the aircraft in conjunction with McDonnell Douglas. There are plans, finally, to take Vertical Take-off and Landing supersonic and even to equip larger aircraft with VTL capacity. For 20 years, the Harrier's virtues remained theoretical, until finally it was given the chance to prove itself. Its future is safe.

BIBLIOGRAPHY

THE LONGBOW

BENNETT, MATTHEW *Agincourt*, Military Campaign Series, Osprey, 1991

CURRY, A. AND HUGHES, M. *Arms, Armies and the Fortifications in the Hundred Years War*, The Boydell Press, 1994

EARL, PETER *Life and Times of Henry V*, Weidenfield & Nicolson, 1972

HARDY, ROBERT *Longbow, A Social and Military History*, J.H. Haynes & Co, 1976

HIBBERT, CHRISTOPHER *Agincourt*, B.T Batsford, 1964

KEEGAN, JOHN *The Face of Battle*, Jonathan Cape, 1976

O'CONNELL, ROBERT *Of Arms and Men: A History of War, Weapons and Aggression*, New York, Oxford University Press, 1989

SCHAMA, SIMON *Landscape and Memory*, HarperCollins, 1995

SUMPTION, JONATHAN *The Hundred Years War*, Faber & Faber, 1990

TAYLOR, F. and ROSKELL, J. translators, *The Deeds of Henry the Fifth*, Oxford University Press, 1975

WYLIE, JAMES HAMILTON *The Reign of Henry V*, Cambridge University Press, 1914

THE BAYONET

BLACK, JEREMY *Culloden and the '45*, Alan Sutton, 1990

COLLEY, LINDA *Britons: Forging the Nation 1707-1837*, Yale University Press, 1992

GRIFFITH, PADDY *Forward into Battle*, Antony Bird, 1981

PREBBLE, JOHN *Culloden*, Penguin, 1967

REID, STUART *A Military History of the Last Jacobite Rising*, Spellmount, 1996; *Like Hungry Wolves: Culloden Moor, 16 April 1746*, Windrow & Greene, 1994

SEYMOUR, WILLIAM *Battles in Britain,1066-1746*, Sidgwick and Jackson, 1975

THE PANZER AND THE T-34

DEIGHTON, LEN *Blitzkrieg: From the Rise of Hitler to the Fall of Dunkirk*, Jonathan Cape, 1979

HARRIS, J.P. and TOASE, F.H. *Armoured Warfare*, B.T. Batsford, 1990

HEALY, MARK *Kursk 1943*, Military Campaign Series, Osprey, 1993

ORGILL, DOUGLAS *T-34: Russian Armour*, Macdonald & Co, 1970

SHEPPERD, ALAN *France 1940, Blitzkrieg in the West*, Military Campaign Series, Osprey, 1990

ZALOGA, STEVE *T-34/76, Medium Tank, 1941-1945*, New Vanguard Series, Osprey, 1994

THE P-51 MUSTANG

DEIGHTON, LEN *Goodbye Mickey Mouse*, Hutchinson, 1982

ETHELL, JEFFREY L. *Mustang: A Documentary History*, Janes Publishing, 1981

ETHELL, JEFFREY L. and PRICE, ALFRED *Target Berlin*, Arms and Armour Press, 1981

FREEMAN, ROGER *The Mighty Eighth: A History of the US 8th Air Force*, Janes Publishing, 1986

GRUENHAGEN, ROBERT W. *Mustang: The Story of the P-51 Fighter*, ARCO, 1976

HESS, WILLIAM *P-51: Bomber Escort*, Pan, 1971

OVERY, RICHARD *Why the Allies Won*, Pimlico, 1995

THE BELL 'HUEY' UH-1

COLEMAN, J.D. *Pleiku: The Dawning of Helicopter Warfare in Vietnam*, St Martin's Press, New York, 1988

KARNOW, STANLEY *Vietnam: A History*, Pimlico, 1994

MOORE, H. and GALLOWAY, J. *We Were Soldiers Once ... and Young*, Airlife 1994

PIMLOTT, JOHN *Vietnam: the Decisive Battles*, Michael Joseph, 1994

SHEEHAN, NEIL *A Bright Shining Lie*, Jonathan Cape, 1989

THE SEA-HARRIER

BRAYBROOK, ROY *Harrier and Sea-Harrier*, Osprey, 1984

BROWN, DAVID *The Royal Navy and the Falklands War*, Leo Cooper Ltd, 1987

COPLIN, J.F. *VTOL Aircraft*, Macdonald & Co., 1967

ETHELL, JEFFREY and PRICE, ALFRED *Air War South Atlantic*, Sidgwick and Jackson, 1983

MASON, FRANCIS K. *Harrier*, Patrick Stephens Ltd, 1981

WARD, NIGEL *Sea-Harrier Over the Falklands; A Maverick at War*, Leo Cooper Ltd, 1992

INDEX